The Edward Curtis Project:
A Modern Picture Story

Marie Clements and Rita Leistner

Talonbooks

Talonbooks
Box 2076, Vancouver, British Columbia, Canada v6b 3s3
www.talonbooks.com

Typeset in Minion and printed and bound in China.

First Printing: 2010

The publisher gratefully acknowledges the financial support of the Canada Council for the Arts; the Government of Canada through the Book Publishing Industry Development Program; and the Province of British Columbia through the British Columbia Arts Council and the Book Publishing Tax Credit for our publishing activities.

Library and Archives Canada Cataloguing in Publication

Clements, Marie, 1962–
          The Edward Curtis project / Marie Clements and Rita Leistner.

Includes play by Marie Clements and photographs by Rita Leistner from photograph exhibition presented in conjunction with staging of the play.
ISBN 978-0-88922-642-5

          1. Native peoples—Canada—Drama. 2. Curtis, Edward S., 1868–1952—
Drama. 3. Leistner, Rita, 1964——Exhibitions. 4. Native peoples—Canada—
Portraits—Exhibitions. 5. Indians of North America—Portraits—Exhibitions.
6. Native peoples—Canada—Pictorial works—Exhibitions. 7. Indians of North
America—Pictorial works—Exhibitions. I. Leistner, Rita, 1964– II. Title.

PS8555.L435E38 2010   C812'.6   C2010-902246-7

The Edward Curtis Project

Play by Marie Clements

MARIE CLEMENTS, ARTIST STATEMENT

I have no artistic statement. Almost nothing left to say. Everything I saw, or wrote, or did, believed and disbelieved, witnessed and perceived, argued and debated, ate and slept is as altered and layered as any truth or dream of being is—it is all in the play.

I asked for it. I brought it upon myself. I invited discourse, love, minus-forty-three-degree weather, plus-forty-three-degree weather, tears, snow and sand, land that moved across my sight for thousands of miles in car window frames, crazy children, deep rain, and strange occurrences. I argued with anyone who had an opinion. I also agreed with those who agreed with me. It was liberating because we were engaged in something other than light and dark, Aboriginal or white, vanishing or surviving. We were making our own pictures out of our own beliefs and they were adding up. We were inside the lies and beauty of history, of gender, and of class, we were making a case for the future, but first we had to see everything, we had to listen across land and nations. So we moved across worlds in small cars, large trucks, planes, boats, and dog sled—a process of getting somewhere.

A collaboration between Edward Curtis, photojournalist Rita Leistner, and me was not an easy thing. All strange bedfellows indeed. But I needed to work with artists I respected, who were deeply committed to their own work and who looked at art as a process, not just a product. I needed to see from all angles because I wanted to know what was behind the picture; to do that, I needed to go in with artists who had the guts and humanity to see it through.

I will be forever affected by what I saw on our "Edward Curtis field trips" because it was on them I saw what I always knew to be true—there is no Vanishing Indian, never was, but for a convenient thought.

We are everywhere and it is beautiful.

I thank you all.

—in spirit, Marie Clements

The Edward Curtis Project premiered January 21, 2010 at Presentation House Theatre, North Vancouver, with the following cast and creative team:

CAST

Kathleen Duborg: CLARA CURTIS / DR. CLARA
Kevin Loring: YISKA / ALEXANDER UPSHAW / HUNGER CHIEF
Stephen E. Miller: EDWARD CURTIS
Tamara Podemski: ANGELINE / PRINCESS ANGELINE

CREATIVE TEAM

Marie Clements: *Co-director*
Brenda Leadlay: *Co-director*
Rita Leistner: *Photographer*
Paula Danckert: *Dramaturg*
Barbara Clayden: *Costume Designer*
Andreas Kahre: *Set & Props Designer*
Bruce Ruddell: *Composer/Arranger/Sound Designer*
Leela Gilday: *Singer/Songwriter*
John Webber: *Lighting Designer*
Tim Matheson: *Projection Designer and Production Photographer*
Jan Hodgson: *Stage Manager*
Karen Griffin: *Assistant Stage Manager*
Kasia Marzencka: *Assistant Director*
Gia Nahmens: *Production Manager*
Liam Kupser: *Technical Director*
Rosemary Georgeson, Rhiana Yazzie: *First Nations Outreach Coordinators*
Brenda and Rose Hanson and Family; Zalmai Zahir: *Translators*
Bonnie McGillvary: *Tour Coordinator*
Richard Wilson: *Northern Videographer*
Susan Roy: *Historian*
Lisa C. Ravensbergen: *First Nations Marketing Outreach Coordinator*

CHARACTERS

1.

EDWARD CURTIS: 1900s. American. 43–63 years old. Photographer, businessman, filmmaker, explorer. At the prime of his life and career.

CHIEF: Edward Curtis's affectionate pet name for himself.

The FATHER: Angeline's father.

2.

ANGELINE: Present. Dene/Russian-Canadian. Early 40s. Journalist.

PRINCESS ANGELINE: 1903. Duwamish. 70 years old. Old daughter of Chief Sealth (Seattle), clam-digger.

3.

YISKA ("After the Dark"): Present. N'lakap'mux/Canadian. Late 30s. Angeline's boyfriend.

ALEXANDER UPSHAW: 1904. Crow translator. Educated at the Carlisle School. In Edward Curtis's words: "The most remarkable man I ever met—perfectly educated and absolutely uncivilized."

THE HUNGER CHIEF: Timeless. A bear-like leader of all peoples and all nations. A shaper of storms and clear skies.

4.

DR. CLARA: Present. Russian-Canadian. Early 40s. Shrink. Feminist.

CLARA: 1900s. American. Early 40s. Edward Curtis's wife and business partner.

STAGING

Music
Traditional and contemporary Native music and American Indianist orchestrations, influenced by time, and wax cylinder recordings and adaptations.

Set
Extremely bare except for walls of light and dark that are able to transform space and time.

Lighting
Carved and sculpted light that reveals and vanishes.

Costumes
Period clothing for both traditional Euro and Aboriginal scenes. Modern clothing for periods in between.

Mediums
Photography, archival film, film, video, archival writing, Euro-Aboriginal, and Aboriginal-Euro orchestral scores, wax cylinders, magic lanterns.

Frame Shift
A matter of focus and perspective that is both physical choreography and photo-manipulation incorporating close up, long shot, wide shot, studio, landscape, and cultural ranges of seeing.

The Picture Story Sequences
In the winter of 1911–12, Edward Curtis toured the continent with his "musicale" or "picture opera," *A Vanishing Race*. It combined photographs, motion pictures, and Henry Gilbert's music. The Carnegie Hall premiere in New York was a resounding success.

The North American Indian Project
Edward Sheriff Curtis began his career as a professional photographer in 1891. His first picture of a North American native was an 1895 portrait of "Princess Angeline" (Kickisomlo), the daughter of Chief Sealth of Seattle. In 1904, J.P. Morgan's daughter-in-law purchased some Curtis photographs at an exhibit in New York. Two years later, Morgan provided Curtis with funding to conduct field-work for a planned twenty-volume illustrated text originally called "American Indians."

The first volume of this monumental work appeared in 1907 under the title *The North American Indian*, with an introduction by Theodore Roosevelt. Curtis himself described the importance and urgency of his work in that first volume: "The information that is to be gathered ... respecting the mode of life of one of the great races of mankind, must be collected at once or the opportunity will be lost."

Though Curtis has often been criticized for staging his photos to recreate an idealized image of American Aboriginal peoples before contact with the colonial culture that was already irrevocably changing their lives, there can be no doubt as to the dedication and commitment Curtis brought to his tireless effort to document what he and his contemporaries considered to be "The Vanishing Indian."

In addition to finally completing the twentieth volume of his epic publication project in 1930, featuring many of his some 40,000 images taken among more than eighty native tribes, Edward Curtis made films and recorded over 10,000 wax cylinders of Indian language and music containing tribal stories and history, wrote short biographies of tribal leaders, and described traditional foods, housing, clothing, games, and ceremonial and funeral customs.

Despite the criticisms that his work was at times staged and therefore "inaccurate," Curtis's ethnographic material remains, in most cases, the only recorded history of "The North American Indian."

The Sun Dance

According to ethnographic, archaeological, and oral histories, the annual Sun Dance ceremony held at the time of the summer solstice has been the most important religious ritual among the many Aboriginal peoples of the Great Plains of North America for millennia. At the centre of the circular Sun Dance lodge, a sacred tree is erected from which families and individual members of the tribe hang sacrificial tokens; in earlier times young men often pierced their bodies to suspend themselves from it as a rite of passage into adulthood; and the dancers, separated within the lodge by barriers or "hedges" into a men's and women's side respectively, to this day embark on vision quests brought about by up to three days of dancing without rest, food, or water. The Sun Dance tree, with its base planted on the ground by a buffalo skull and its topmost branch singed by a ritual fire symbolizing the sun, though unique to the North American prairie, has many close analogues among the so-called "shaman's trees" central to ancient rituals stretching from Northern Europe to Siberia.

The ceremony is used to honour the cycle of the four seasons, to give thanks for the yearly return of the great buffalo migrations, to recite the individual and family stories of power that create and maintain the relations between members of the community, to celebrate the sacred interdependence of all living beings, and to offer totems and make sacrifices to the creator. It is said that Sitting Bull, too old to participate as a warrior, sacrificed forty pieces of his own flesh at the Sun Dance ceremony at the time of the battle of the Little Big Horn.

SUBTITLE SLIDE: "PRELUDE"

Lights fade up on ANGELINE's fingers as her body lies almost suspended on an empty floor. Her fingers begin to move like she is playing a piano. She hits a note. Then another. The notes combine oddly into—

MUSIC: "A Snow Lullaby"—Leela Gilday

The notes build clearly and beautifully as the light exposes more of ANGELINE, wrapped in a blanket on the floor. Her eyes open as she wakes from a deep sleep. Family pictures begin to develop on the dark walls surrounding her.

ANGELINE

My mother's walls were filled with pictures … evidence of our success as a family … unit. Smiling children. Two girls. One older. Clara. One younger. Me. A handsome mother. A beautiful father. Mixed-race marriage. Contemporary.

She looks around at the pictures.

ANGELINE

We posed like all families pose. Arranging ourselves … until we began to understand with age … our poses had always been pre-arranged.

A picture of her mother smiling.

ANGELINE

Lee Anne, my mother … smiling. She died last year … Isn't she beautiful?

As she speaks, she writes a caption for her mother's picture on the floor:

SLIDE CAPTION: "Lee Anne, mother, Dene-Saulteaux"

A picture of her father, hunting rifle in hand, standing beside an upside-down deer.

ANGELINE

Steve, my father, hunting defenseless animals.

As she speaks, she writes a caption for her father's picture on the floor.

SLIDE CAPTION: "Steve, father, Russian descent"

A picture of her psychiatrist sister, sitting in her office, appears. She gets up and walks towards it.

ANGELINE
My sister Clara … a doctor … a shrink, that is … trying to look above normal.

As she speaks, she writes a caption for her sister's picture on the wall.

SLIDE CAPTION: "Dr. Clara, daughter of mixed marriage …"

She looks intently at her sister's picture and then continues to write.

"Rather white-looking"

She looks over at a picture of herself developing up. In the picture, she is wearing the same dress she wears now, and is holding an award. She walks towards the developing portrait, inserting herself into the picture, into the frame as "Snow Lullaby" begins to slowly distort through.

ANGELINE
Me … accepting an award today … For a story … a story I was the first to break. I was up north covering the Arctic Games … I was up north—

SFX: The sound of her newscast builds under: "This just in from the far north … Three Aboriginal children were found frozen to death in the snow as temperatures plummeted to the minus-forties and their father, age 24, was found drunk. Treated for frostbite and hypothermia, the children's father said his youngest daughter was sick, so he had ventured out to get help and got lost in an icy field … The father told his sister at some point … he dropped the kids …

ANGELINE
This was supposed to have been a great night. A perfect picture.

She tries to get out of her award image as the newscast begins to drown her. Finally disengaging herself from the frame, she backs away hardly able to breathe as:

SFX: The sound of a family celebration dinner becomes louder.

Her sister approaches her, carrying a large wrapped book.

DR. CLARA
Look who's up … We thought you were going to sleep the night away. I've been dying to give this to you …

ANGELINE
Why didn't you wake me?

DR. CLARA
You fell asleep … you seemed so tired, we thought it was better you get your beauty rest …

ANGELINE
You think I need it?

DR. CLARA gives her a hug and a kiss …

DR. CLARA

Supper's almost ready … oh … you're freezing.

*DR. CLARA grabs ANGELINE's hand to take her to the table and
ANGELINE drops it. DR. CLARA continues to move towards the dinner
table, where her FATHER and YISKA sit.*

ANGELINE

I don't feel cold …

*DR. CLARA stops and looks back at her. Her FATHER and YISKA look
up. They barely move.*

ANGELINE

I don't feel … anything.

SFX: The sounds of the Arctic begin to seep in under.

ANGELINE

I was standing there, my skin beginning to burn, burn, with a cold
beginning … frozen I could see the details without the distraction of caring.

*A shutter and flash. ANGELINE looks back at the table that begins to
stutter. She looks intently at her FATHER.*

ANGELINE

My father's handsome face … he has always been so charming, so charming it
can hurt.

A shutter and flash. ANGELINE looks at her sister.

ANGELINE

My sister's flawless porcelain skin.

A shutter and flash. ANGELINE looks at her boyfriend.

ANGELINE

My boyfriend's dark eyes that see everything.

*A shutter and flash. YISKA looks up at her, suddenly concerned. She
writes his caption.*

SLIDE CAPTION: "Yiska, my boyfriend, N'lakap'mux"

*A shutter and flash begin to stutter in a choreography of family dinner
poses that are surreal, stuttering in reality and still frames.*

Shutter. Flash. Frame.

ANGELINE

I looked at them—and all I wanted to do was get out. Get out of the picture
that was made for me—get out of the picture I had made for myself. Get out of
all the lies that have framed me.

Shutter. Flash. Frame.

FATHER
>   Angeline?

>   *YISKA appears before her, oddly dressed in a parka.*

YISKA
>   Angeline?

>   *She looks at her father and then at YISKA, far away.*

ANGELINE
>   I'm just going to/

>   *Shutter. Flash. Frame.*

FATHER
>   /For God's sake, Angeline, come sit down and join us … we've been waiting for
>   hours … I'm starving/

>   *DR. CLARA gets up and moves towards her.*

DR. CLARA
>   /Angie?/

>   *ANGELINE looks at her FATHER.*

ANGELINE
>   /Are you?

>   *Pause. Her FATHER looks at DR. CLARA for help.*

>   *ANGELINE begins to move away slowly.*

ANGELINE
>   I'm not feeling well … I think I need to lie down …

>   *YISKA gets up and walks towards her.*

ANGELINE
>   You can't stop me.

YISKA
>   Angeline? Where are you? Come back …

ANGELINE
>   You need to let me go.

>   *DR. CLARA grabs her arm.*

DR. CLARA
>   Angie?

>   *ANGELINE moves from her touch and, backing away from the others,
>   removes her shoe.*

ANGELINE

I took my shoe off. Just one. I took the heel … the heel of my shoe, the heel … like a pointer really pointed to get a point across to a blunt world …

DR. CLARA

Angie … it's alright …

ANGELINE

No, it's not … nothing's alright … Nothing is alright.

ANGELINE freezes, her hand gripping the shoe like a weapon. She moves towards them, raising her heel, then takes aim at their image and hits, shattering the picture.

SFX: The sound of glass breaking and falling.

Shards of glass fall to the ground like crystals.

ANGELINE

I think when they really think about it … they will be relieved I released them from me. I know I felt better. I feel better.

She smiles for a moment.

ANGELINE

I felt better …

Blackout. A long beam of light drives down, lighting a sliver of ANGELINE's face.

ANGELINE

It's beautiful, don't you think? … How the light hits you so purposefully just before you will never be seen again …

She smiles.

ANGELINE

My sister thinks I am having a breakdown but she doesn't know everything … I am having a … break … through … I am breaking through …

Hands move into the light. Her FATHER hands her a crucifix, YISKA a rock, DR. CLARA the large wrapped book. She begins to unwrap the book. She looks down at it, then laughs as she holds it up.

ANGELINE

My family has been showing up, leaving … odd … things out of nowhere.

She smiles.

ANGELINE

My sister gave me this book by Edward Curtis. It is heavy. *The North American Indian.*

She flips through the pages.

ANGELINE
It didn't make me feel better …

She opens to a page and looks in.

ANGELINE
But I at least, I found a caption in the darkness I can identify with—

*MUSIC: ORCHESTRA PRELUDE: "By the Arrow," String Intro.—
Henry Gilbert*

She writes a caption for herself that appears below her.

CAPTION: "The Vanishing Indian"

*She opens the book and begins to read as she is lit like a beautiful Edward
Curtis photograph.*

ANGELINE
"Age upon age, generation upon generation, they have slowly eroded their
social structure. The Crucible of time has developed their primitive laws to a
protection against their own weakness."

SLIDE: A young, dashing Edward Curtis.

SLIDE CAPTION: "E.S. Curtis, 1899, Self-portrait"

*She looks over as a portrait develops up towards its full glory, almost
coming alive as EDWARD CURTIS begins to speak.*

EDWARD CURTIS
Proud, arrogant in their imagined superiority, disdainful of civilization's
strength, which they cannot comprehend. Fools! They knew not with what they
reckoned. Advancing civilization has crushed all before it; primitive man can
but snap and snarl like a brute cur at the giant which has been his destructor …

EDWARD CURTIS walks towards her in the dark.

EDWARD CURTIS
The buffalo are gone; the human brother is but a human fragment, robbed of
his primitive strength, stripped of his pagan dress, going into the darkness of
the unknown future …

ANGELINE looks up in the light as his dark hands touch her face softly.

EDWARD CURTIS
So said E.S. Curtis …

*His hands covering her face with gentleness, the lights slowly fade
romantically to darkness.*

ANGELINE
(*from the darkness*) Finally a darkness that has my name on it.

An unknown darkness takes over the space. It is entirely dark.

FRAME SHIFT.

MUSIC: "By the Arrow" cont.—Henry Gilbert

SUBTITLE SLIDE: "PICTURE STORY I: Carnegie Hall, New York, 1911"

A stereo-optical illusion comes into focus, highlighting a now-standing EDWARD CURTIS, age 43, as he appears in his prime, ready to engage his audience.

The rich backdrop of Carnegie Hall fades up: dark gold and auburn, Greek pillars, and grandness.

SUBTITLE SLIDE: "The Vanishing Indian"

SUBTITLE SLIDE: "by Edward Curtis" joins the title.

SLIDE: Edward Curtis photograph of horses and Indians going into the darkness.

SLIDE CAPTION: "The Vanishing Race, Navaho, 1904"

SFX. The sound of thunderous applause.

EDWARD CURTIS stops and looks out into the audience. He poses, adjusting his face in the light for effect.

EDWARD CURTIS

Thank you. Thank you indeed … it is a fine evening, a fine introduction.

He lights a cigarette.

EDWARD CURTIS

My greatest desire tonight is that each and every person here enter into the spirit of our evening with the Indians. We cannot weigh, measure, or judge their culture with our philosophy. From our analytical and materialistic viewpoint theirs is a strange world. Deity is not alone in a world of universal voice, universal spirit. I want to see this beautiful, poetic, mysterious, yet simple life, as I have grown to see it through the long years with the many tribes. Toward that end let us close our eyes for an instant, and in a flash of time span the gulf between today's turmoil and the far away enchanted realm of primitive man. We have entered what is to us a strange land. Man and nature are one and a-tune. All about us are the mysteries of the Infinite.

FRAME SHIFT.

SUBTITLE SLIDE: "FIELD WORK I: The West, 2008"

MUSIC: "Let the Rest of the World Go By"—J. Keirn Brennan and Ernest R. Ball

SFX: The sound of soft rain.

SFX: The sound of a pill bottle falling to the floor and pills rolling.

Lights up on ANGELINE as she sits on the floor, reaching for the pill bottle and spilled pills in the darkness.

The hand of EDWARD CURTIS reaches inside her light and offers her the pill bottle, then the spilled pills. He stands just outside her light, looking down.

ANGELINE
I'm having a bad day … or maybe it's a bad night. A bad year maybe? One day. One night. One year. All the same, really.

EDWARD CURTIS
Do the pills help?

She shrugs.

ANGELINE
Pills do what they are supposed to do …

She takes the pills out of the bottle and into her palm.

ANGELINE
… they take the edge off reality, putting me in control of my own numbness.

He hands her a glass of water.

EDWARD CURTIS
A small consolation, I suppose.

She swallows the pills and as she looks down, the light expands to include the room with EDWARD CURTIS in it. She watches as he looks at her home.

ANGELINE
You're … the photographer?

EDWARD CURTIS
I've retired actually.

ANGELINE
Believe me, nobody retires from who they are … It's admirable to try, but not worth the effort.

EDWARD CURTIS
Is that right?

ANGELINE
That's the way I've come to understand it.

EDWARD CURTIS
That seems so ominous … no wonder you look so down.

ANGELINE
They call it depression. It makes me want to lay my head down but the angle doesn't stop me from thinking … Have you ever been depressed?

EDWARD CURTIS
Off and on/

ANGELINE
/For how long?

EDWARD CURTIS
My whole life.

ANGELINE
Reassuring.

He offers his hand and pulls her up. They sit at a table, where a bottle of Scotch and two glasses have been left.

EDWARD CURTIS
I was in Seattle one time, in a deep black fog barely able to get out of bed. But I said to myself, get up and go for a walk, that will clear your head. So off I went, walking in the streets. Suddenly I heard birds, and a beautiful light just happened from the clouds and then there was music. Music? I turned towards the music but it had no face. I looked down and looking up was the face of a cripple strapped to a wooden board on wheels. I looked at him playing the accordion. Playing the accordion? I figured if that man could put his soul in his music from down there. I would not give up either.

He offers her a smoke.

ANGELINE
I don't smoke.

She takes it anyway. He lights her cigarette and then his own.

EDWARD CURTIS
Me neither.

ANGELINE
What should I call you?

They sit and smoke.

EDWARD CURTIS
People close to me call me Chief.

ANGELINE
Seriously?

He nods and takes out a journal from his inside coat pocket. He begins to write.

CHIEF
I'm going to call you/

SLIDE CAPTION: "Primitive Indian Wom …"

ANGELINE
/Aren't you going ask me what I call myself?

CHIEF
I wasn't going to … but if you think it's important.

ANGELINE
I do … I do.

*She takes his journal and pen, crosses out the "Primitive Indian Wom …"
and writes.*

SLIDE CAPTION: "Most Beautiful Woman You've Ever Met"

ANGELINE
I call myself "Most Beautiful Woman You've Ever Met."

CHIEF
Please …

ANGELINE
It only seems fair if I have to call you Chief …

She motions to pour him a drink.

CHIEF
Fair enough … I don't drink.

She pours him a drink anyway. She pours herself a drink. They cheer.

ANGELINE
Me neither.

They drink in silence.

ANGELINE
On second thought, just call me Angeline … "Most Beautiful Woman You've
Ever Met" is a lot to live up to … And if I were you, I would reconsider
"Chief" … for the same reasons …

The SLIDE CAPTION disappears. He looks at her.

CHIEF
Are you married?

ANGELINE
Living together … Trying.

His face screws up slightly.

CHIEF
Yes … there is always trying.

ANGELINE
Did your break-up hurt?

CHIEF
Why do you think my marriage broke up?

ANGELINE
> Because you look pained.

He doesn't answer.

ANGELINE
> Or constipated.

CHIEF
> Pardon me?

ANGELINE
> You look pained … as in your marriage caused you pain … or you look like you are having a hard time passing something … constipated.

CHIEF
> Thank you for the clarification. Let's talk about something else …

ANGELINE
> Fine.

He lights another smoke.

CHIEF
> Are you hungry?

ANGELINE
> I'm always hungry.

CHIEF
> Would you like me to fix you something? I'm an excellent cook.

ANGELINE
> Seriously? How humble.

He gets up and removes a portable stove from his bag.

CHIEF
> Don't be a wisehead …

ANGELINE
> Alright … How attractive …

CHIEF
> Better.

He assembles cooking utensils from the darkness.

ANGELINE
> I have some buffalo in the freezer. I've been keeping it for a special occasion.

CHIEF
> It is a special occasion … to meet a writer.

ANGELINE
How did you know I was a writer?

CHIEF
Anybody who wants to rewrite something I wrote is usually a writer.

ANGELINE
Or an Indian.

Pause.

CHIEF
What did you say?

She doesn't respond. He smiles.

CHIEF
I forgot how good it feels to cook for someone.

He turns his back towards the stove.

FRAME SHIFT.

SLIDE: Prairie field.

ANGELINE looks up as a yellow sun bears down around her. Gradually a yellow prairie takes over the space, rolling as far as the eye can see.

From far away, YISKA appears, drumming. He begins to sing a traditional song on the open prairie.

MUSIC: Traditional song—YISKA sings.

ANGELINE looks at him and then stands on the chair. Raising her body up to get closer to the sky.

YISKA turns around and looks at her.

YISKA
I'm praying for you.

They look at each other.

FRAME SHIFT.

DR. CLARA
What are you doing?

ANGELINE turns her head to the sound of her sister's voice as the prairie disappears suddenly and she is left standing on a chair.

ANGELINE looks over at DR. CLARA's voice just inside the darkness. DR. CLARA enters her office as framed university degrees begin to appear on the walls.

ANGELINE
Who's asking?

DR. CLARA
Who do you think?

ANGELINE smiles.

DR. CLARA
I asked you to wait in my office ... I thought you might be climbing the walls but I didn't think you'd be climbing the chairs ... get down ...

ANGELINE
No ... I like the view.

DR. CLARA looks around and sees only darkness.

DR. CLARA
That's an expensive chair ...

ANGELINE
Would it be alright if it was a cheap chair?

DR. CLARA
Get down ...

ANGELINE
No.

DR. CLARA
I think it's only fair ... if you're in someone else's room you play by their house rules.

ANGELINE shrugs.

ANGELINE
Stupid people follow stupid rules ...

DR. CLARA
Get down.

ANGELINE
No.

They just look at each other. ANGELINE stretches herself towards the sky.

ANGELINE
Do you ever wonder what it would feel like to stretch yourself so fully to the sky you become a part of it? Just raise yourself above the petty shit of perfectly placed furniture, and all the things that look so right but are so fucked ... Detach yourself from all the things you can't fix. All the things that don't make sense but should.

She breathes into the sky.

ANGELINE
Standing here like this above yourself … you see land so flat it's hard to know
where the sky ends and the land begins, where you begin and end. You see
everything because you are a part of everything and there is nothing you don't
know …

FRAME SHIFT.

*The CHIEF turns around from carving the buffalo into steaks. His hands
bloody, he stops and looks at her.*

CHIEF
/You're right. You're right.

ANGELINE sees him. They smile.

ANGELINE
You understand?

CHIEF
Yes, I understand.

FRAME SHIFT.

DR. CLARA
Angie?

ANGELINE keeps looking at the CHIEF. He finally turns towards his cooking.

DR. CLARA
Angie …

ANGELINE finally looks at her.

DR. CLARA
What did you do today?

ANGELINE gets down from the chair, deflated.

ANGELINE
I came here to "do" lunch.

DR. CLARA
I wanted to talk to you/

ANGELINE
/Talk./

DR. CLARA
/to you because I want you to see a colleague of mine/

DR. CLARA hands her a business card.

ANGELINE
/Very tricky/

DR. CLARA
/Dr. Wilson. I set up an appointment/

ANGELINE
/I didn't agree to this …

DR. CLARA
How unusual …

ANGELINE *hands back the card.*

ANGELINE
I'm fine.

DR. CLARA
You're a mess.

ANGELINE
Is that a professional opinion, or a personal one?

Pause.

DR. CLARA
Both.

They look at each other.

ANGELINE
Thanks.

DR. CLARA *looks down.*

DR. CLARA
I'm sorry … I'm just worried about you …

ANGELINE
You make me tired. I think I'm just going to lie down on your couch …

DR. CLARA
… Angie?

ANGELINE
I'm okay … people need to lie down after they've been standing on a chair for a long time … it's normal.

DR. CLARA
Normal.

DR. CLARA *covers her sister with a blanket.* ANGELINE *looks up as a framed family portrait begins to fade up on the wall.*

SLIDE: *Sears Studio portrait of Dr. Clara, her husband, son, and two daughters, circa 1996.*

SLIDE CAPTION: *"Big C, Ted, and kids"*

ANGELINE
You still have that photo up.

Pause.

DR. CLARA
Ancient history.

ANGELINE
Is it?

DR. CLARA
It's 1996, for Godsakes, look how heavy I was.

Pause. DR. CLARA walks towards her family portrait. She touches her husband, adjusting his jacket lapel. She looks right at him.

DR. CLARA
I'm finally going to ask him for a divorce.

ANGELINE
I'm sorry …

She backs away slightly and looks at her children.

DR. CLARA
It's time … we haven't lived together in years …

ANGELINE
You still love him? … Or just the idea of him?

She looks at ANGELINE.

DR. CLARA
Maybe I still love the idea of *us.*

Pause. They both look out into the darkness.

FRAME SHIFT.

MUSIC: "The Night Scout"—Henry Gilbert

SUBTITLE SLIDE: "PICTURE STORY II: Carnegie Hall, New York"

A stereo-optical illusion comes into focus. The rich backdrop of the theatre fades up: dark gold and auburn Greek pillars and grandness surround EDWARD CURTIS as he continues his lecture series.

Dissolving, flickering SLIDE SEQUENCE I–VI: I, "The Vanishing Race, Navaho, 1904"; II, "The Hunkalowanpi 'Offering the Skull'"; III, "The Indians of the Palm Canyons and Cactus Plains"; IV, "The Apaches"; V, "The Hopi and Snake Dance"; VI, "Evening in Hopi Land."

EDWARD CURTIS
Tonight we go to the land of the Indian, and as in other travels, let us glance at the scope of the project. First, what is an Indian? The American Indian is one

of the five races of man, and of this race there are yet to exceed fifty linguistic stocks in North America. When I say that—I mean just that—languages fundamentally differing. Of dialects there were at one time of the discovery fully one thousand in North America. Passing through the linguistic groups, let us glance at the life and manners. We have natives of the subtropics dwelling beneath the waving palms in the land of perpetual warmth, and, to the contrary, natives of the Arctic directing their frail skin crafts among the dangerous icebergs. And between these extremes are countless tribes, all, according to habitat, differing in cultures.

MUSIC: "The Night Scout"—Henry Gilbert, adapted by Bruce Ruddell

SLIDE: Edward Curtis photograph of a man standing on the open land in a buffalo robe.

SLIDE CAPTION: "For Strength and Vision, 1904"

YISKA, dressed in a large buffalo robe, turns from the photograph.

He looks at EDWARD CURTIS. They stare at each other for a long time not moving, barely breathing.

SFX: The sound of a wax cylinder recording under—

YISKA
(*in Peigan*) I am not for your eyes … lower your need to see what is not for you. I am not for your eyes. Step backwards and I will erase your footprints on my spirit. Step backwards one clumsy foot at a time, backwards towards your own knowing. I am not for your eyes. Stay where I cannot see you and you cannot see me. Let us stand that way, our eyes lowered for the good of all men and all gods.

EDWARD CURTIS steps back slowly, slowly, slowly.

FRAME SHIFT.

MUSIC: "Let the Rest of the World Go By"—Words and music by J. Keirn Brennan and Ernest R. Ball, adapted by Bruce Ruddell

SUBTITLE SLIDE: "FIELD WORK II: The West, continued"

SFX: The sound of rain.

The CHIEF turns and appears. He lights a cigarette.

CHIEF
Did I tell you I saw the Sun Dance back in 1900 on the Plains with the Peigans? I saw it and it changed me so entirely it remapped the course of my life.

ANGELINE
You saw it?

CHIEF
I saw it. I wasn't supposed to … You don't believe me?

ANGELINE

I believe you believe it.

CHIEF

Do you believe that in that instant—a chance encounter changed my past and my future? … Does that sound odd?

ANGELINE

No. Chance encounters can do that.

He sets down a pot of buffalo stew and brings a salad to the table, setting it for two with ease. He smells the stew.

CHIEF

I wrote about it … the Sun Dance … Like many things I have seen, I was the first white man to write about it. To take a picture so no one would ever forget they were here …

ANGELINE

Amazing … This is really good stew/

CHIEF

/Thank you … The Snake Dance, Hopi. The Yeibachi Dance, Navajo, etcetera, etcetera … They thanked me for taking it … for preserving it forever …

ANGELINE

Did they … Did they really?

CHIEF

Do you want to know why? Because pictures are … realities.

ANGELINE

Are they? Or are they just perceptions? And if so, of whom? Those who take the picture or those who pose for them?

He pauses and takes a bit of meat.

CHIEF

If I'm not mistaken, the same could be said for a writer …

ANGELINE

The difference is I don't write pretty words … I don't write words people want to dress in … You do.

CHIEF

People don't see me as a writer.

ANGELINE

But you did write. You wrote word pictures and your pictures were word.

CHIEF

I saw it. I photographed it. I wrote about it. It's not that complicated.

SLIDE: Lights fade up on a portrait of Clara Curtis. They both watch as CLARA fades up and breathes into herself.

SLIDE CAPTION: "Clara Curtis, 1914"

ANGELINE
No, it's not … It's beautiful.

He looks at the photo and then reaches down and lights another smoke.

CLARA
Edward?

He doesn't address her as she moves into the space and towards blue water developing in a basin. She immerses her hands in the water as a beautiful Edward Curtis photograph develops up.

FRAME SHIFT.

SLIDE: An Edward Curtis photograph of a Kutenai canoe on a lakeshore dissolves up, surrounding CLARA.

SLIDE CAPTION: "Kutenai Girls, 1910"

MUSIC: "Kutenai Country"—Henry Gilbert

CLARA smiles as she looks at the picture.

CLARA
Edward, it is so picture perfect, I can almost hear the bottom of the canoe as it hits the mouth of the water   . the oar as it touches the glass surface …

She looks over and then turns to the darkness, almost shyly towards him.

EDWARD CURTIS
A crackerjack picture to be sure.

She smiles.

CLARA
Edward, you did hear me.

He hesitates, not looking at her, and then exits. She hears his footsteps trail off.

CLARA
Perhaps not.

FILM: She watches as the Kutenai canoe animates and moves across the water in frames.

CLARA
Where did poor Clara go? She went on a canoe across a great lake.

She laughs and then looks down.

CLARA

I wish to lower my hands off the sides of the canoe and let my fingers touch the bulrushes that reach up to me, touching my hands so lightly, so right … if only to interrupt my sad story for a moment …

MUSIC: "Kutenai Country"—Henry Gilbert, adapted by Leela Gilday

SLIDE: The eyes of a Kutenai girl fade up under the dark surface of the water in the basin. Her hair fades up in long black strands.

CLARA looks down into the basin of dark water and watches as ANGELINE takes over the image. CLARA cups the water with her hands, pouring it over ANGELINE's hair, affectionately.

CLARA whispers closer to ANGELINE's ear.

CLARA

Your dark eyes look back into me for days on end … and I wish to tell you everything that is left unsaid. Undone. Unloved. Maybe secrets can exist between us …

She looks out.

CLARA

Secrets can exist between those that are only seen for convenience.

CLARA looks down again, changed. She talks softly, but her hands become tense, as do her words as she chokes them out.

CLARA

But here there is only one secret worth saving … do you hear me? I will always be his wife … the mother of his children … his partner … but you … you in the end will be nothing but the memory of an Indian.

CLARA takes her hand and covers ANGELINE's mouth and pushes her face back into the water.

ANGELINE struggles against her force and then submerges under the water. There is a long silence as CLARA backs away from the basin, wiping her hands on her white apron, backing away into the darkness as:

MUSIC: "Kutenai Country"—Henry Gilbert, adapted by Bruce Ruddell, strings

ANGELINE suddenly gasps up from the wet darkness.

ANGELINE

I wish to rise from the roots of bulrushes … I wish to rise from the roots of bulrushes … I wish to feel the water … feel the water … feel the water …

YISKA appears from the darkness, reaching her across space, calling out to her, his words getting closer …

YISKA

Open your eyes, Ange … open your arms … look at me …

ANGELINE

> I can't.

YISKA

> You can.

He appears, finally taking her in his arms.

YISKA

> (*in Kutenai*) I wish to rise from the roots of bulrushes … take my clothes off, every stitch … feel the water like ice on my skin and rise to the shock of being touched by a god that has many names … I wish to be free of all things I am not and will never be …

She opens her eyes.

YISKA

> Sleeping in water … What were you thinking?

ANGELINE

> I just closed my eyes for a minute … do we have to do this right now?

YISKA

> No.

ANGELINE

> Perfect.

Pause.

YISKA

> Do you wanna talk about it?

ANGELINE

> I have an appointment to talk with someone professional … Clara's arranging it/

YISKA

> /Just like she's arranged the drugs …

She gives him the look.

YISKA

> Fine.

She picks up a pack of smokes and takes one out. He gives her the stop-smoking look.

ANGELINE

> Stop looking at me.

He approaches her.

YISKA

> You're smoking again …

He takes the cigarette from her hand.

ANGELINE
I don't smoke.

YISKA
Right.

He looks at her.

ANGELINE
Really … I feel better … I'm on a plan … everything is looking up.

YISKA
Really?

She smiles. He touches her face.

YISKA
Liar.

A long pause. She stares at him and turns from him coldly.

ANGELINE
I wish you'd just leave … How long you going to hang in there? You're fucking everything up … I'll smoke if I want to … Why can't a person smoke if they want to? … Why can't a person die if they want to? … Why can't they just lay down and die if they want to without having to fucking explain every fucking detail … I just want to die … alright … there …

He moves towards her.

YISKA
You can't say that … don't you dare say that … don't you ever say that to me again …

She begins to cry.

ANGELINE
I'm sorry …

YISKA
You can't keep doing this … do you understand me? You can't …

ANGELINE
I'm sorry … I'm sorry for everything …

He looks at her.

ANGELINE
I'm sorry.

YISKA
You're safe with me, Ange …

ANGELINE

Am I? You say I am but when you get tired of dealing with it you will look away and I won't be able to find your face.

He bends to her.

YISKA

My face is right here. My face is here, Ange … you just have to look.

ANGELINE

What do you want me to say? What do you want me to do? Tell me.

He reaches out to her and touches her face, her lips. He places his hand on her eyes.

YISKA

You don't have to say anything. You don't have to do anything. You just have to be … here. You just have to be here.

They kiss and begin to make love.

The CHIEF stands from a distance and watches, taking out his lens. He looks at the scene and then, taking the lens away from his eye, looks on.

EDWARD CURTIS

I wish to rise from the roots of bulrushes … take my clothes off, every stitch … feel the water like ice on my skin and rise to the shock of being touched by a god that has many names … I wish to be free of all things I am not and will never be …

FRAME SHIFT.

SLIDE: An Edward Curtis photograph of whaling fades up.

SLIDE CAPTION: "The Captured Whale, 1915"

MUSIC: "Haida War Song"– Haida Chief Guujaaw

FILM: Fades up in full greys. Whales begin to appear throughout the grey, appearing and submerging … appearing and submerging …

SFX: The sound of whales.

EDWARD CURTIS closes his eyes and shifts, shifts, like a man hearing something below himself that is large.

CLARA approaches him softly as he talks. He doesn't acknowledge her, but allows himself to be undressed. She removes his shirt and his pants, being mindful of his bad hip. He is left wearing only his long johns, through.

CHIEF

Did I ever tell you the time I was hunting whales with the Haida? An extraordinary field trip … great big swells the size of mountains … taking the boat up and down, climbing and then crashing and then right beside you like a monster from a different world—a whale … crashing down on the boat … unbelievable strength and grace … coming down on you, coming down on you like a hammer, spraying you with air and water, coming up and then again crashing down on the boat, crashing down on the men, crashing down on me, on this hip trying to break me … break me in two.

She looks right at him.

CLARA

I miss you.

He looks down at his journal.

CHIEF

I miss you too, Clara … I miss you …

He continues to write as she stands and then leaves the space.

CHIEF

Love to you and the children, kindest regards, I am … sincerely yours, E.S.C.

The CHIEF gets up and looks over at ANGELINE sleeping. He takes a lens out of his pocket and looks at her intently, framing her.

FRAME SHIFT.

MUSIC: "Let the Rest of the World Go By"—Words and music by J. Keirn Brennan and Ernest R. Ball, adapted by Bruce Ruddell

SUBTITLE SLIDE: "FIELD WORK III: The West, continued"

SFX: The sound of rain.

Suddenly ANGELINE looks up at the CHIEF. He smiles and puts the lens back in his pocket. She smells the air. It smells like coffee.

CHIEF

I made some coffee. Do you want a cup?

ANGELINE nods. He stands with a coffee pot and cups. He pours them coffee and lights another cigarette.

ANGELINE

It smells good …

She looks at the coffee pot.

ANGELINE

I don't recognize the coffee pot …

CHIEF

Oh, it's mine. I travel with it everywhere. I don't like taking chances with my coffee. It's important if you travel a great deal to … put out the little things that make you feel at home … Smoke?

He lights a cigarette and passes it to her. They smoke.

CHIEF

My father was a Baptist minister, did I tell you that?

ANGELINE

I read it somewhere …

CHIEF

I travelled with him out West, preaching the word of God.

ANGELINE

Did you believe any of it?

CHIEF

It was enough that he did. He believed it with a wondrous zeal that consumed him … I think perhaps I inherited the zeal.

ANGELINE

Not the light of God.

CHIEF

No … just the belief in light … but I suppose the belief in darkness too. That intense darkness transforms what your naked eye sees into what it could only imagine holding. If light is the basis of photography … maybe darkness is the basis of humanity.

She smokes.

ANGELINE

Hmmm … The small circle, the glass, you carry … in your pocket …

CHIEF

My father gave it to me when I was a boy … a stereoscopic lens from a camera he brought back from the Civil War.

ANGELINE

You carry it everywhere with you?

CHIEF

Yes … A reminder to see everything as if it is for the first time.

The CHIEF gets up and cracks a few eggs in the frying pan.

CHIEF

Are you hungry?

ANGELINE

No, thank you. I have to get dressed today. I have an appointment, which means I should do something with my hair.

CHIEF

I might be able to help with that.

The CHIEF opens his bag and pulls out a few long black wigs. He places one on her head.

ANGELINE
I'm not going there alone.

He puts a black wig on. They laugh.

YISKA appears in his underwear, looking at them. The CHIEF continues laughing, but extends his hand.

CHIEF
People that know me call me Ch/

YISKA just looks at him, giving him the eye.

CHIEF
/I mean Edward … Ed, if you like.

YISKA
I don't like.

He looks at ANGELINE.

YISKA
Who's this?

ANGELINE
You can call him Ed if you like.

YISKA
I don't want to call him anything …

ANGELINE gives him the look. The CHIEF approaches.

CHIEF
Can I ask you your name?

YISKA
No.

ANGELINE
People call him Chief too.

CHIEF
A pet name?

YISKA glares at him.

ANGELINE
No, because he is one …

CHIEF
I see …

YISKA
Do you?

The CHIEF looks at him. YISKA looks back.

CHIEF
You remind me of someone …

The CHIEF looks confused for a minute.

YISKA
We all look the same … don't worry about it …

CHIEF
I had a friend a long time ago, a translator I worked with whose name was Alexander … Upshaw.

YISKA
Let me guess … he was Indian.

The CHIEF goes about cooking eggs and bacon.

CHIEF
An educated Indian. Crow. He had gone to the Carlisle School. He graduated and went on to become a leader of his people. An educated Indian/

YISKA
/You said that/

CHIEF
/loved by his own people, hated by whites. He died young … a tragic death … he died before his promise.

He dumps a couple of eggs on a plate and hands it to YISKA.

YISKA
Tragic. Do you have any bacon with that sunny side up?

CHIEF
Yes I do … Yes I do …

The CHIEF scoops a couple of strips, happily serving them to YISKA.

CHIEF
You from around here?

YISKA puts the bacon in his mouth and nods with a full mouth.

CHIEF
What do you do?

YISKA
I'm a translator of Aboriginal languages at the university.

The CHIEF watches him, then takes out his lens and begins to frame him and ANGELINE.

CHIEF

What kind of Chief are you?

YISKA

The real kind. You?

CHIEF

It's a name of affection given to me because I worked and lived with so many Indians … over many/

YISKA

/How touching …

The CHIEF lowers his lens briefly.

CHIEF

Are you upset?

YISKA

No, do I look upset? … I feel crowded. You ask too many questions.

CHIEF

Occupational hazard. Sorry. I guess it is hard to separate what you do from who you are.

YISKA

Listen … I don't like waking up to strange men … on my own land, if you get what I am saying … especially those who talk too much and get things from my fridge.

He pauses.

CHIEF

I'm just passing through.

YISKA looks at all of him.

YISKA

Nobody who looks like you passes through without taking everything he can.

LIVE PICTURE PORTRAIT: YISKA freezes in his pose.

FRAME SHIFT.

SLIDE: An Edward Curtis photograph of ALEXANDER UPSHAW in a bone breastplate fades up as YISKA breathes into it.

SLIDE CAPTION: "Alexander Upshaw, Crow"

CHIEF

I'm sorry, I didn't mean/

ALEXANDER UPSHAW

/He's asking you why you are here. He doesn't trust you ... just so that you know ... he doesn't trust no white man, no how, no way and no bacon and egg is going to change that. Some things a frying pan can't fix. Sometimes a translator has to speak even when two men are speaking the same language.

CHIEF

I am a patient man. Good things come to those that are patient. He'll like me sooner or later.

ALEXANDER UPSHAW

You are a stubborn man. A gun comes to those that are stubborn. Or a knife, maybe, in the small of the back. Trust me ... you always gotta watch the curve of a dark road ... it can go either way.

The CHIEF lights another cigarette and smiles.

CHIEF

I always said you were perfectly educated and absolutely uncivilized.

ALEXANDER UPSHAW laughs. The CHIEF smiles and then looks intently at the photo of YISKA. He moves slightly this way and that, uncomfortable.

ALEXANDER UPSHAW

You are worried. Then worry. A man should worry ... I should have worried more. I married a white woman because I had the taste of her tongue on my voice. I was walking as any man has a right. I was walking home and then there, just a movement in the darkness that you know is no good, then no good comes into me like a knife ... bleeding then, dying then. There.

CHIEF

He's looking at me. His eyes are following me.

ALEXANDER UPSHAW

Get used to it. All Indians have to have eyes on their backs.

The CHIEF looks deeply into YISKA's eyes in the picture.

FRAME SHIFT.

He looks back and ALEXANDER UPSHAW freezes as the portrait and then vanishes.

FRAME SHIFT.

He looks back at YISKA, who has returned to his body.

YISKA looks over at CLARA, who is crying as she wipes up water from the floor.

YISKA
>Shouldn't you be with your own people? Your own family?

>*FRAME SHIFT.*

>*MUSIC: "Clara's Song"—Bruce Ruddell*

>*EDWARD CURTIS walks toward her.*

EDWARD CURTIS
>Clara, are you alright?

>*She doesn't respond immediately. She wipes her eyes with her wrists and looks up, pretending she hasn't been crying.*

CLARA
>Yes. Yes. I am fine. My hands are deep in Indians, as yours, and getting deeper.

>*She grabs a towel and wipes her hands.*

CLARA
>I'm surprised … Why the sudden concern?

EDWARD CURTIS
>Don't be like a cross child, Clara. I've come to talk. Obviously you feel there is something wrong.

CLARA
>You haven't been home for months.

EDWARD CURTIS
>We've had this conversation.

CLARA
>Then start a new one.

>*He just looks at her.*

EDWARD CURTIS
>What I want is to come home and not have to deal with this drama every single time … I want/

CLARA
>/I want.

>*He stops.*

CLARA
>I want. It sounds strange to say it out loud. I want.

>*She smiles, clipped.*

CLARA
>Did you ever ask me what I wanted? Did you ever ask? "Clara, my love, my wife, mother of my children, my partner … What is it that you want?"

EDWARD CURTIS

You knew from the beginning what it was going to be like.

CLARA

Did I? With all the lies of the future untold, how does anybody know what it is going to be like …

EDWARD CURTIS doesn't say anything.

CLARA

I want … more … I want more. In case you were going to ask now. I want more. Abstinence from existing makes a person hungry.

She looks at him.

CLARA

And I am so hungry. I could eat you …

EDWARD CURTIS

I don't understand.

She turns away.

CLARA

Then by all means cook an omelette and pat yourself on the back …

EDWARD CURTIS

I'm sorry I didn't hear you.

She turns to him.

CLARA

When have you ever heard me?

EDWARD CURTIS

I am not going to stand here and listen to this.

CLARA

Then sit.

Pause. He looks at her.

EDWARD CURTIS

I don't have time for this, Clara.

She gathers her words.

CLARA

But you have time to gallop around the country doing your Indian lectures, dining with presidents and society women, raising money, raising money for what? One more book. One more field trip …

She looks at him directly.

CLARA
The women. You think I don't see the women, Edward? … Am I to pretend it's all just rumour? … What strange bedfellows will you lie with next?

It is incredibly still as his eyes turn hateful.

EDWARD CURTIS
You have offended me with such allegations. You have offended my cause, my work, my very being.

CLARA sits down slowly, suddenly weighted.

CLARA
Lie down with them all for all I care, Edward. Lie down … What does any woman know of her husband's passions? … All she needs to understand is that they don't include her.

She turns cold.

EDWARD CURTIS
Are you finished?

CLARA
Yes, I believe I am. I am. I want a divorce.

She looks up at him.

CLARA
Who would have thought I could say it?

EDWARD CURTIS sits down heavily in a chair, stunned.

FRAME SHIFT.

CLARA looks up and walks towards a beautiful life-size image of a young EDWARD CURTIS.

SLIDE: Edward Curtis portrait.

SLIDE CAPTION: "Edward Curtis, 1899"

She strokes his face and leans in to kiss his lips. The picture doesn't respond.

FRAME SHIFT.

ANGELINE continues looking at all the framed degrees as they appear on the wall. DR. CLARA turns.

DR. CLARA
What are you doing here?

ANGELINE
You took the picture down. Good for you.

DR. CLARA
Thanks … you're supposed to be at your appointment.

ANGELINE
I got all dressed up but couldn't make myself go.

DR. CLARA
Then you should have called me and I could have cancelled.

ANGELINE
Why did you give me the book?

DR. CLARA
It just makes me look bad.

ANGELINE
Always worried about appearances.

ANGELINE picks up a framed certificate.

DR. CLARA
What book? Put that down.

ANGELINE
Scared I'm going to break it?

DR. CLARA
No ... Yes.

ANGELINE plays with the frame, moving it from hand to hand.

ANGELINE
Let's try again ... Why did you buy me the book?

DR. CLARA
I'm not in the mood ... Alright ...

She looks at ANGELINE, who isn't budging.

DR. CLARA
Because I thought you would enjoy it.

ANGELINE
I'm trying to get my head together and you thought I would enjoy looking at beautiful pictures of "vanishing Indians."

DR. CLARA
It was just a gift to show you I cared. Edward Curtis was a photojournalist of sorts and you're a journalist ... It's a coffee-table ... book. You put it on your coffee table ... if you had one.

ANGELINE
This is how you care ... because this is how you think.

She looks at the framed certificate with a golden seal.

ANGELINE

Wow, you've adopted a starving black kid from Africa for what—$30.00 a month—and put it on your wall. Impressive … I mean, maybe I should donate some money to Africa … or at least fuck Bono/

DR. CLARA turns away.

DR. CLARA

/Maybe I shouldn't have framed it …

Pause.

ANGELINE

I thought for a minute you were going to say, "Maybe I shouldn't have fucked Bono."

ANGELINE smiles. Long pause.

ANGELINE

You know what would be really impressive framed on your wall? A golden certificate saying you donated money to starving kids in your own country.

Pause. ANGELINE doesn't say anything.

DR. CLARA

Point taken.

Pause.

ANGELINE

Really.

DR. CLARA moves towards ANGELINE and takes the framed certificate from her.

DR. CLARA

Is it the photographs that have gotten to you?

ANGELINE

The photos are so beautiful I am barely able to breathe.

DR. CLARA

Have you been able to write?

ANGELINE shakes her head.

DR. CLARA

It must be hard … You're not just any writer, are you? You're a foreign correspondent … an Aboriginal foreign correspondent … in your own country … hired by the biggest national newspaper to cover Aboriginal issues … in your own country …

ANGELINE

Stop saying "in your own country" … it's freaking me out.

Almost crying, ANGELINE looks away.

DR. CLARA
Look at me … What's wrong?

ANGELINE
Everything.

DR. CLARA
Can you be more specific?

ANGELINE
No.

SFX: The faint sound of children playing in the snow.

ANGELINE
Everything is not the way it should be. It's like I'm still lying in the snow and everything looks so beautiful.

She looks up.

ANGELINE
I can hear them … you know? I can hear them … Sometimes when I put my hand out I can touch them. If I leave they will be so alone, Clara, so alone … and it's so cold …

She closes her eyes and begins to hum and then sing.

MUSIC: "Snow Lullaby"— ANGELINE sings.

FRAME SHIFT.

YISKA appears from the darkness and puts his arms around ANGELINE. He joins her in the song. She opens her eyes.

ANGELINE
I didn't write the whole story.

YISKA
You wrote the facts. You wrote what you were expected to write.

Pause.

ANGELINE
Did I? I didn't write the real story …

She doesn't wait for his response.

YISKA
Ange …

ANGELINE
I wrote that an Indian father was drunk and dropped his three kids in the snow …

YISKA

He did …

ANGELINE

Did he? Or did we drop him a long time ago? I should have written that the father of those children was so young, so poor … living in a house that was so contaminated it should have been torn down … living between cardboard walls with no food, no clean water, no phone, no heat, and the only reason he decided to go out into minus-thirty-eight weather was because one of his kids was sick … He went out to get help … Do you think it was all his fault? Or maybe we all should own a little piece of it?

YISKA

We do, Ange, because we've survived, but most people don't want to hear the whole truth … they don't want to see it, they just want us to disappear.

She gets small.

YISKA

You have to find a way to keep going.

ANGELINE

Are you scared I will die?

YISKA

(*in Salish*) I am afraid I would die without you. I am afraid I would die.

She looks at him.

ANGELINE

I am afraid to live.

YISKA

If we stand here like this, just the two of us … then we balance the whole world out.

ANGELINE

Say it in my language.

YISKA

(*in Dene*) If we stand here like this … just the two of us, then we balance the whole world out.

They stand, not moving.

FRAME SHIFT.

SUBTITLE SLIDE: "PICTURE STORY III: Carnegie Hall, New York, 1911"

A stereo-optical illusion comes into focus. The rich backdrop of the theatre fades up: dark gold and auburn, Greek pillars and grandness.

MUSIC: "The Signal Fire to the Mountain God"—Henry Gilbert

Dissolving, flickering SLIDE SEQUENCES VII–XII: VII, "The North West Plains Life"; VIII, "North Pacific Coast Tribes"; IX, "The Kutenai of the Lakes"; X, "Invocation to the Buffalo"; XI, "The Mountain Camp"; XII, "On the Shores of the Pacific."

Edward Curtis photographs project on ANGELINE and YISKA, who begin to animate them. They look at EDWARD CURTIS throughout.

EDWARD CURTIS

The first and greatest problem before all human beings is that of food, and naturally the culture of any group is largely determined by this. Students of primitive religion will tell you that the question of food is first thought in a majority of religions systems. This admitted, let us look at it in relation to the Indian. We pass from the proud buffalo hunting Indian to the less favoured … I have asked you to take this broad glimpse at the Indian subject that you have firmly in mind that we cannot refer to the Indian as a unit, as is often done, but rather we must in a measure consider each group as a … nation … a project unto itself.

EDWARD CURTIS watches as the Indian photographs seem to become more and more real.

EDWARD CURTIS

There is an erroneous impression perhaps fathered by our own presumption in considering our reaching out to the Infinite to be religion, and the Indian's like act to be heathenism.

The INDIANS look straight back at him, their eyes following him.

EDWARD CURTIS

They are looking at me … Stop looking at me …

He looks out at the audience.

EDWARD CURTIS

I'm sorry, sometimes my eyes play tricks on me … where was I now? …

He looks down at his papers.

EDWARD CURTIS

Rather than being without religion, every act of his life was according to divine prompting. True, the gods bore strange names, but the need was as great, the appeal as devout … the appeal as …

He looks over at the images as they begin to blur and stretch to a water-like surface that flickers over the space. The MUSIC begins to stutter and stop out of sequence.

EDWARD CURTIS

There is a problem … Can we just stop … until we have solved the … Stop that projector … it's … I'm sorry we seem to be having technical difficulties … let us take a short break. A short breath. Thank you.

He wipes the sweat from his face and smiles.

EDWARD CURTIS
Can we have some music for our friends? There is music … my mistake …

He gestures and music plays under.

EDWARD CURTIS
Intermission. Thank you … for your understanding.

He turns to gather himself and in doing so sees the film of CLARA.

*FILM: A small canoe begins to make its way across the projected water.
CLARA sits inside the canoe, looking into the water.*

EDWARD CURTIS
Clara?

*FILM: CLARA drops her hand into the lake and leans in towards the
water, as if touching the other side. EDWARD CURTIS is rattled …*

EDWARD CURTIS
Please, God … don't make it wet. Please, Clara …

A small light on ANGELINE.

CLARA
I had a dream I was moving across the lake, like I'd done a million times
before. I stopped just then by chance almost, my reflection perfect. Strong.

ANGELINE
From what I could see she was quite beautiful. Auburn hair. Fair skin. She was
wearing a white blouse and a long skirt.

CLARA
I was wearing a beautiful hat …

ANGELINE
She was waiting … A kind of waiting that made me sad because she was
looking into the water, seeing everything that she had lost … and not looking
away.

EDWARD CURTIS
She was my wife. My wife. My partner. The mother of my children.

EDWARD CURTIS looks at ANGELINE.

ANGELINE
I know.

From the darkness.

FRAME SHIFT.

DR. CLARA appears from just outside the darkness.

DR. CLARA
You look sad.

ANGELINE
I hate sad people … it's so privileged.

DR. CLARA
What did you say?

ANGELINE turns towards her.

ANGELINE
Maybe we're so privileged it has made us sad.

DR. CLARA just looks at her.

ANGELINE
If we were all sinking in a boat right now … Who do you think would get out first?

DR. CLARA
I don't know … you're acting weird.

ANGELINE
Seriously … who do you think would get out first? You've seen the movie—a big fuckin' indestructible boat filled with rich people filling their gaps, a drunk captain, an iceberg … the music plays—If both of us were on the same boat, but different levels, who do you think would get out first? You or me?

DR. CLARA
It would depend on chance. Life depends on chance and circumstance/

ANGELINE
/Chance?/

DR. CLARA
/Circumstance. Survival/

ANGELINE
/And survival depends on the chance of your skin being white or brown?

DR. CLARA
You're twisting things …

ANGELINE
Because they are twisted … Aboriginal people are at the bottom of the boat … and everyone else is in first class fighting to get on a life raft while the music plays. I'm not saying they don't feel sorry for taking all the life rafts … that's what the music is for … I'm just saying … the movie never changes … When is the movie going to change?

DR. CLARA
I don't know what you are talking about.

ANGELINE
Sure you do. You do, because you would be in the first dinghy, wouldn't you?
… First dinghy, Clara.

DR. CLARA
We have the same blood. The same history …

ANGELINE
But not the same colour of skin, so not the same reality. You are an onlooker
who has the ability to feel sorry for someone while remaining tight-fisted.

DR. CLARA
And what are you?

ANGELINE looks at her wall of degrees.

ANGELINE
So many degrees and yet you have so little depth. You are dimensionless.

She looks at DR. CLARA.

DR. CLARA
What are you? What are you in all this? Please clarify it for me … so
complicated, so complex, so brown?/

ANGELINE
/Say it./

DR. CLARA
/So fucked up.

DR. CLARA looks down, about to apologize.

ANGELINE
At least I never left my children for a white man to raise.

DR. CLARA ices.

DR. CLARA
What did you say?

Pause.

ANGELINE
What am I?

ANGELINE closes her eyes and smiles oddly.

ANGELINE
I am nothing.

DR. CLARA
Angie?

ANGELINE
I can smell peaches. Can you smell them? I can smell the wind and it smells like peaches.

DR. CLARA stares at her sister.

FRAME SHIFT.

YISKA watches the CHIEF as he rummages madly through his stuff looking for his journal. YISKA begins to circle him.

YISKA
Leaving so soon.

EDWARD CURTIS
I was just getting my things together.

YISKA
Your things?

EDWARD CURTIS
Yes, my belongings.

YISKA
You missing anything?

EDWARD CURTIS
Yes ... I seem to have misplaced my journal and some photographs I have taken on this trip.

YISKA approaches them.

YISKA
You mean these?

YISKA has his journal in his hand. He takes the photos from the middle of journal and passes the journal to the CHIEF.

CHIEF
Yes ... I would like my photos back.

YISKA
Even if they are of us ... they are still yours.

CHIEF
Please ... my photos ...

YISKA turns deadly cold. He rips the photos in half ... they fall to the ground.

YISKA
I want you to get out before I kill you ... I want you out. I want you gone.

CHIEF
Is that right?

*YISKA advances on the CHIEF threateningly. The CHIEF pulls out a gun
shakily and points it at YISKA. YISKA stops.*

YISKA

You fuckin' … fuckin' … I should wring your scrawny fuckin' …

CHIEF

This is no joke. No joke. A serious affair.

YISKA

No one's laughing here, Chief.

CHIEF

You were going to scalp me and I had to take matters into my own hands.

> *YISKA looks at them.*

YISKA

What are you talking about?

EDWARD CURTIS

I've been in this situation before. When I was living with the Sioux—a Sioux
warrior pulled a knife on me because he didn't want me to take any more
pictures. I knew I'd seen you before.

YISKA

I'm not Sioux. Put the gun down.

CHIEF

Not until you put your knife down.

> *YISKA shrugs.*

YISKA

I don't have a knife.

EDWARD CURTIS

Indians always have a knife.

YISKA

I don't have a knife.

EDWARD CURTIS

Have it your way … just don't get close to me or, so help me God, I will shoot
you.

> *The CHIEF motions with his gun to the journal and torn photographs.
> YISKA steps closer and leaves them on the table. The CHIEF waves
> YISKA back. He looks over his stuff and tries to piece the pictures together.*

YISKA

Do you think that the Indians you took pictures of thought you were actually
taking pictures of them?

CHIEF

What are you talking about?

YISKA

You were taking pictures of your idea of them. Big difference.

CHIEF

They understood the power of art, so they understood me, and I understood them.

YISKA

Did they understand the ramifications of being frozen in time without the possibility of seeing what survival looks like?

CHIEF

Academic babble.

The CHIEF puts the journal in his jacket. YISKA moves towards him. The CHIEF motions with the gun for YISKA to stay where he is.

CHIEF

I don't like you.

YISKA

I've never liked you.

Pause.

CHIEF

I don't get it. I've been nothing but cordial to you since I arrived, and from the very beginning you looked at me like I'm one of them.

YISKA begins to get closer

YISKA

You are one of them.

CHIEF

I held high views of the North American Indian ...

YISKA

Get off the pedestal ...

CHIEF

I dedicated my life ... over thirty years of my life documenting the North American Indian, my health, any money I made, any hope of lasting happiness.

YISKA

And we are grateful ...

CHIEF

I stood up for them ...

YISKA gets closer.

YISKA
When it suited you … when everything suited you …

CHIEF
I asked you to step back and put the knife down! I warned you …

The CHIEF raises his gun.

YISKA
Spoken like a true Custer.

CHIEF
Don't you dare … don't you dare compare me to that long-hair! Put the knife down!

YISKA looks at him and mimes putting a big knife down.

YISKA
I am putting the almighty scalping knife down! Chief!

Pause.

YISKA
What are you going to do now, Chief, shoot me?

The CHIEF begins to crumble. YISKA approaches him.

YISKA
Shoot me, Chief, and get it over with.

They stare into each other.

YISKA
What, you think you can cook a pair of eggs and everything is fine?

The CHIEF lowers his gun, ready to explode.

CHIEF
Yes … yes, I do … I do … because it has to be! I cooked for them, and I cooked for them, and I cooked for them … do you want to know why? Because I couldn't stand watching them starve to death over and over and over … everywhere I went … starvation, death, incarceration, hunger … They were so hungry I would cook for them every chance I got … every goddamn chance I got … Goddamn it! Goddamn, Goddamn it to hell!

He stops and looks at YISKA, trying to reel himself in, barely breathing, almost crying.

EDWARD CURTIS
I smell peaches.

FRAME SHIFT.

DR. CLARA

You think that because you are fucked in the head … you can say anything you want …

ANGELINE

I'm sorry … I'm sorry, Clara … I didn't mean to/

DR. CLARA

/They wanted to stay with him. So … they stayed with him.

She tries to smile, to breathe.

ANGELINE moves towards her.

DR. CLARA

No … no.

DR. CLARA moves from her.

DR. CLARA

Do you want to know the thing I miss the most? I miss putting them to bed. Having the blankets pulled up to their little chests. They are so warm and small. You bend down into their little necks, just below their ears, and your cheek touches theirs, and you kiss them then … hesitating before you rise because what you wanted, what you really wanted all along was to smell them. To smell them because it smells like …

ANGELINE

Peaches.

DR. CLARA

Like peaches …

DR. CLARA closes her eyes. ANGELINE closes her eyes.

FRAME SHIFT.

EDWARD CURTIS closes his eyes. YISKA closes his eyes. They all stand in a pose as Canyon de Che fades up, leaving them in a peach grove.

SLIDE: Across the backdrop, an Edward Curtis photograph of the beautiful Canyon de Che fades up in oranges.

SLIDE CAPTION: "Canyon de Chelly-Navaho, 1904"

YISKA

Like peaches planted in the most unexpected of places …

YISKA closes his eyes and begins to sing.

MUSIC: YISKA sings.

EDWARD CURTIS

Across the worlds I went. I was only frightened when I was scared. In the deep red canyon down where green peach trees grow despite themselves, just before dawn, a baby is trying to be born. I camped there in the valley not yet understanding that my very presence was a curse. A curse once spelled to the wind can never be taken back. A baby was trying to be born, stuck, they said because of me. Stuck between flesh and spirit, between surviving and vanishing. Because of me they said. Because of me just being somewhere a white man had never been. Were they right? Does it matter? Were they wrong? It doesn't matter. Was it real? It was real … real as that baby's cry finally lifting into a wind that smelled of ripe peaches … reaching me, telling me … its first day will allow me to live another. Telling me to never forget … never forget … the balance between being killed or saved is but a child's struggle to breathe and the belief of one man over another.

YISKA

(*in Dene*) If we stand here like this we balance the whole world out.

They all stand, not moving, breathing in the moment.

The sand of the desert begins to rise under the feet of the following scenes, swirling.

EDWARD CURTIS begins to move. YISKA looks at him and whispers a warning.

YISKA

Don't move.

EDWARD CURTIS takes his lens out and raises it to his eye.

YISKA

One day. One night. One year.

FRAME SHIFT.

EDWARD CURTIS turns and looks over.

SLIDE: Desert sand swirls and settles, forming the west coast shore, fog rising through.

SLIDE: An Edward Curtis portrait of Princess Angeline fades up as she bends down on the shore, collecting clams.

SLIDE CAPTION: "Princess Angeline, 1902"

PRINCESS ANGELINE

(*in Salish*) It's hard to believe in another day when you are hungry.

SFX: The sound of the tide grows louder.

EDWARD CURTIS looks over at the portrait.

FRAME SHIFT.

ANGELINE bends up from the portrait as PRINCESS ANGELINE, age 70.

EDWARD CURTIS moves towards her, relieved to see an old friend.

EDWARD CURTIS

Is that you, Princess? Is that you? I can hear you like I can hear the sea … a tide coming in like a whisper leaving behind nothing and everything … cold at my feet with the shock of a clock that is wet … I saw you there bending down, putting your hands in the deep sand, reaching down in, and pulling up spitting clams. And then later on the side of the street, crouched down, head up staring into a horizon that was us, white and moving forward. I said then … Are you Princess Angeline, daughter of Chief Seattle?

He looks over. PRINCESS ANGELINE does not look at him.

EDWARD CURTIS

You said nothing … such is the state of any princess.

He walks closer to her.

EDWARD CURTIS

I walked closer and again I said … are you Princess Angeline, daughter of the great Chief Seattle?

She smiles slowly.

EDWARD CURTIS

You didn't look up, but smiled. I was man enough to know … a smile is at least a door.

He bends down to her level.

EDWARD CURTIS

Can I take your picture? A picture. It meant nothing to you. A picture.

He brings his lens to his eye.

FRAME SHIFT.

SLIDE: An Edward Curtis portrait of Alexander Upshaw.

SLIDE CAPTION: "Alexander Upshaw, Crow"

YISKA appears as ALEXANDER UPSHAW.

ALEXANDER UPSHAW

(*in Salish*) He wants to take your picture?

She turns and looks at the translator.

PRINCESS ANGELINE

(*in Salish*) Why?

ALEXANDER UPSHAW

(*in Salish*) That is what he does.

PRINCESS ANGELINE
(*in Salish*) That is what he does with his pretty white hands. Me, my hands like crow's feet are bent and salted. Me, my hands are old and smell like the bottom of a great water. Tell him yes … if he has any food to spare.

She looks down at her rusted and salted hands.

PRINCESS ANGELINE
(*in Salish*) Me, my hands are tired of being hungry … diggin' … diggin' … diggin' even in my sleep diggin' for food that is nothing more than a hard shell.

EDWARD CURTIS
What does she want?

ALEXANDER UPSHAW looks at her for a long time.

EDWARD CURTIS
Alexander, what does the squaw want?

He looks back at EDWARD CURTIS and, making a decision, stands in a formal stance.

ALEXANDER UPSHAW
Money. The daughter of the great Chief Sealth wants one dollar a picture. The daughter of the great Chief Sealth will not pose for less than one dollar a picture.

EDWARD CURTIS looks at her, amazed by the request.

EDWARD CURTIS
Tell her that is too much. What does she think I am made of?

ALEXANDER UPSHAW looks into the eyes of the old princess. She puts her hand out.

PRINCESS ANGELINE
(*in Salish*) Food.

He hesitates and then bends to her with honour and a soft voice.

ALEXANDER UPSHAW
(*in Salish*) You will make him a great man by letting him take your picture and for this great honour he is going to give you a dollar a picture.

He looks over at a puzzled EDWARD CURTIS and makes his play.

ALEXANDER UPSHAW
She thinks that you must be a great man to be able to capture the very image of her soul.

EDWARD CURTIS puffs up ever so slightly.

ALEXANDER UPSHAW
For this she agrees that a dollar would be an equitable trade between artists. So it is done.

EDWARD CURTIS extends his hand towards the princess hesitantly.
They shake.

ALEXANDER UPSHAW
Congratulations, sir, you have made your first transaction with an Indian …
your first picture.

EDWARD CURTIS reaches inside his pockets.

CHIEF
Yes … I have … Yes, I did …

EDWARD CURTIS lays a silver dollar in her weathered hand.

*He goes to draw away and she grabs his hand suddenly and looks right
into him.*

PRINCESS ANGELINE
Where do you think you're going?

Shutter. Flash. Frame.

Stunned EDWARD CURTIS stands looking at her for a long time.

PRINCESS ANGELINE
Did you capture my soul, or did I capture yours? Maybe I am still inside you?

*PRINCESS ANGELINE begins to laugh and as she does she becomes a
portrait.*

SLIDE: Edward Curtis studio portrait of Princess Angeline.

SLIDE CAPTION: "Princess Angeline, Duwamish—People of the Inside"

PRINCESS ANGELINE
(*off-stage*) Diggin' … diggin' … diggin' … for food that used to be a feast and
now is nothing more than leftovers … You have made me hungry.

Shutter. Flash. Frame.

FRAME SHIFT.

*EDWARD CURTIS begins to move backwards slowly as sand begins to
rise sifting and shaping in swirls.*

*The HUNGER CHIEF fades up suddenly, wearing a bear's robe. He
stands before the water. Bending down, he takes water in his hands,
wiping his face and hair wet. He looks up and into EDWARD CURTIS.
He moves towards him.*

EDWARD CURTIS
I am afraid … What do you want from me? I've nothing left.

HUNGER CHIEF
Then you are finally one of us. The only way a white man can become an
Indian is to starve. You want to come inside … You want to live with the

Indians, then you must die with us. Come inside … come inside. Come inside our belly.

Parts of Edward Curtis Indians begin to develop up as negative images, captured in and out of the fog. Shots of spirits emerge and move forward.

The HUNGER CHIEF removes a large knife from his suede belt and approaches EDWARD CURTIS directly.

Shutter. Flash. Frame.

The HUNGER CHIEF cuts a strip of EDWARD CURTIS's clothing away, then another … as real and unreal Indians begin to multiply in the action of becoming bare.

EDWARD CURTIS
I am afraid …

EDWARD CURTIS is left standing almost naked.

HUNGER CHIEF
I am afraid …

The INDIANS stand with the HUNGER CHIEF.

INDIANS
I am afraid.

Hundreds of Edward Curtis Indians from different tribes are projected behind the HUNGER CHIEF.

Shutter. Flash. Frame.

The INDIANS breathing into themselves begin to move towards him, forcing EDWARD CURTIS backwards as they transform through.

HUNGER CHIEF/INDIANS
I am and remain thin. I want to eat. We want to eat. I don't want to be sick. I want to get well.

Shutter. Flash. Frame.

EDWARD CURTIS
I am and remain thin. I want to eat. We want to eat. I don't want to be sick. I want to get well.

Shutter. Flash. Frame.

HUNGER CHIEF/INDIANS
I wish you'd go. I wish to go. I go to the houses. A man is coming to the house.

They lay their hands on him, pushing him back.

EDWARD CURTIS
Don't make it wet.

They look into him.

I pretend to be sick. I pretend to eat. I'm not sure I am sick. That food makes me sick. It is he who saved me. I think of him. I think of you.

EDWARD CURTIS
There are teeth inside me, inside the pit of me gnawing, gnawing nothing because there is nothing to consume. Eating flesh that is mine to get out. Eating me from the pit of my belly, from the pit of my being.

The INDIANS push him back, close to the edge of the water. They hold him before the water.

HUNGER CHIEF/INDIANS
I just got sick. I am very poor. I am very rich, weak, strong, short, tall, fat, skinny, dead, blind, thief.

Shutter. Flash. Frame.

They look at him accusingly.

HUNGER CHIEF/INDIANS
You are a thief ...

Shutter. Flash. Frame.

The INDIANS hold him before the water. They grab him.

EDWARD CURTIS
I am not a thief. I think of me. I think of you. Don't make it wet. Please, God, don't make it wet.

They put him in the water.

HUNGER CHIEF/INDIANS
We eat together. I am going to put you into the water, midnight, an ore, black clouds, salt, something bad, something different, one night, one day, one year ... We eat together.

EDWARD CURTIS sinks down into the lake. The INDIANS begin to disappear as they submerge in the water.

HUNGER CHIEF
I am going to put you into the water, midnight, an ore, black clouds, salt, something bad, something different, one night, one day, one year ...

A white-faced CLARA appears before him.

EDWARD CURTIS
Clara? Is that you? I see you, Clara ... I see you ... I truly see you ... finally ...

She reaches him and finally touches every inch of his face. Her hands paint his face white.

EDWARD CURTIS
I'm sorry. I'm sorry, I ... forgive me ... forgive me.

She leans into him and kisses him full on the mouth. They freeze.

FRAME SHIFT.

The sandstorm winds down softly, settles, then begins to build as the HUNGER CHIEF bends down and wipes clear a patch of earth that has turned to ice. He picks up the frost and snow and throws it in the air. A blinding snowstorm builds through.

ANGELINE appears in the middle of the storm. She looks at him as white silhouettes of modern-day Indians blur in and out of the blizzard.

HUNGER CHIEF
I am afraid …

Shutter. Flash. Frame.

INDIANS
I am afraid.

Shutter. Flash. Frame.

ANGELINE
I am afraid.

Shutter. Flash. Frame.

HUNGER CHIEF/INDIANS
I am and remain thin. I want to eat. We want to eat. I don't want to be sick. I want to get well.

They move towards her slowly, then stand around her.

ANGELINE
I am and remain thin. I want to eat. We want to eat. I don't want to be sick. I want to get well.

Shutter. Flash. Frame.

HUNGER CHIEF/INDIANS
I want to be warm. I want to be well. I want to live.

ANGELINE
Don't let them be frozen.

HUNGER CHIEF/INDIANS
I want to drink clean water. I want to be warm. I want to love. I want to live. I think of them. I think of you.

ANGELINE stops and bends over.

ANGELINE
I am cold … so cold. They are inside me, inside the pit of me gnawing, gnawing until there is nothing. Eating flesh that is mine to get out. Eating me from the pit of my belly, from the pit of my being.

Shutter. Flash. Frame.

Shutter. Flash. Frame.

Shutter. Flash. Frame.

HUNGER CHIEF/INDIANS
I just got sick. I am very poor. I am very rich, weak, strong, short, tall, fat, skinny, alive, blind, dead …

ANGELINE
We are not dead. I think of them. I think of you. Don't make them frozen. Please God, don't make them frozen.

HUNGER CHIEF/INDIANS
We eat together. I am going to put you into the storm, bright sun, white, blue clouds, breath, something bad, something different, one day, one night, one year … We eat together.

They stand as the whiteness begins to dissipate and the Arctic fades through.

ANGELINE looks around at the landscape. ANGELINE watches as the INDIANS and the HUNGER CHIEF disappear slowly.

HUNGER CHIEF
(*off stage*) We eat together. I am going to put you into the storm, one day, a light, bright sun, tears, something bad, something different, one day, one night, one year. We eat together.

SLIDE CAPTION: "Arctic, 2008"

EDWARD CURTIS and DR. CLARA stand wrapped in blankets. YISKA in his parka. They stand in the snow.

YISKA
There was a call around 4:00 in the morning …

DR. CLARA
There was a call …

EDWARD CURTIS
A call that rang throughout the village …

DR. CLARA
A call you don't want to hear because you know it's not good.

YISKA
I picked up … probably every house in the village picked up and set out into the night that is day/

EDWARD CURTIS
/Day that is night.

ANGELINE

I set out like everyone else, blankets in hand … The sun was just coming up or down … it was beautiful. Like nothing could touch the way it looked … I walked through the snow … slower … less able to walk in deep snow … less able to keep up with those that have been doing it all their lives … they passed in front of me like a wave of bodies and breath that clung to the air. I was behind but I was also able to see things for the first time. Seeing so clearly I could hear …

YISKA

A young father had been found in the snow … almost frozen …

EDWARD CURTIS
Almost frozen …

YISKA

Drunk … and then thawing … asking where his three kids were.

YISKA

"Where are my kids?"

DR. CLARA
"Where are my children?"

YISKA

They weren't in his house. They weren't in any home.

EDWARD CURTIS
They weren't in any home. They weren't in any house.

SFX: The faint sound of children's voices singing …

ANGELINE

But there was a sound … A kind of a beautiful sound that found me, and I looked down …

YISKA

They were outside.

SLIDE: A baby impression in the snow.

ANGELINE freezes and stumbles toward the baby's impression.

ANGELINE

Frozen. She froze in minus thirty-eight degrees. In a small sweater. A small pink sweater. I kept thinking … Jesus Christ … Jesus Christ …

She stumbles forward.

SLIDE: A larger impression of a boy in the snow appears.

ANGELINE

I stepped forward … and there … five steps in the snow … another child, age 4, frozen … these beautiful, rosy, chubby cheeks … Jesus Jesus Christ … I stepped back.

EDWARD CURTIS

One day. One night. One year.

She falls back.

SLIDE: A larger impression of a girl in the snow appears.

ANGELINE

I stumbled back … when my hand landed … landed on something solid but soft … Jesus, no … no … I looked back and her hand was reaching out as if she had seen something … a possibility, age 8. She reached out and froze in that possibility …

DR. CLARA

One day. One night. One year.

ANGELINE shakily takes out her notepad and pen and tries to write.

ANGELINE

I knew it was too late because they were so beautiful. Perfect. Frozen in time. Dead … I begin to write … "Three children were found in the snow …" And that's as far as I got … Three children were found sleeping …

She begins to take her outer clothing off and lays it on the snow.

ANGELINE

I began to sing a song my Aunt Ruth used to sing to me when I was a child

YISKA

One day. One night. One year.

MUSIC: "Snow Lullaby"—Leela Gilday

ANGELINE

As I sang … I began to take my coat off … the layers I had put on … I took off and I put them on their little bodies … It was so cold … and they were so alone … I laid down with them, covering them with a blanket the best I could … I rocked them into their sleep, tucking them in … into their sleep … shhhh … baby … I'm here … I'm sorry, I'm sorry, I'm so … so sorry this happened to you … I became so tired … I could barely keep my eyes open … because I was so sorry so tired … so I shut my eyes … I shut them … so I shut my eyes … because I could no longer see what I could no longer know.

ANGELINE looks up, covered in a blanket of snow. She looks directly at EDWARD CURTIS.

ANGELINE

Aren't you going to take the picture? … take the picture … if vanishing is so beautiful … take the picture … take the picture … if vanishing is so … beautiful …

EDWARD CURTIS pauses and looks at her.

EDWARD CURTIS

I can't take the picture … I can't take the picture, Angeline … because I am not alive. You are.

EDWARD CURTIS begins to freeze in his pose.

CAPTION: "Edward Curtis, 1868–1952"

EDWARD CURTIS fades and vanishes.

FADE OUT.

MUSIC: "A Snow Lullaby"—Leela Gilday

SUBTITLE SLIDE: "EPILOGUE"

Lights fade up on ANGELINE's fingers as she lies in the snow.

SFX: From the distance, sled dogs bark.

ANGELINE

I heard the sound of dogs barking and the sled scraping the surface, snowshoes on this world made of ice. I hear. I heard voices and finally a shadow above me all tall-limbed into the sky.

YISKA

Angeline …

He reaches her and bends down to her, gathering her.

She opens her eyes into his.

ANGELINE

Take me back, I said. Take me back … I am ready. I am ready to see everything. Please.

She touches his face. He pulls her into him.

YISKA

Touch me … Remember me … Smell me … Look at me, Ange, … love me and we can move forward … Do you hear me? … love me and we can move on but you have to see me, Ange … you have to see love because it is the only thing we have that can't be starved from us.

ANGELINE and YISKA stand.

ANGELINE

We have survived despite what you can, or cannot, see.

YISKA

We have survived despite what has or hasn't been said/

ANGELINE

/What has or hasn't been done …

Photographs from The Edward Curtis Project *field trips begin to appear on the walls around them.*

YISKA

One day. One night. One year …

ANGELINE

… We have survived across time, across place, to love each other towards a new day.

SUBTITLE SLIDE: "The Edward Curtis Project, 2007–2010"

The Edward Curtis Project

Photographs by Rita Leistner

The exhibition component of *The Edward Curtis Project* opened, in conjunction with the premiere of the play, at the North Vancouver Museum at Presentation House, North Vancouver, on January 21, 2010 as part of the Vancouver 2010 Cultural Olympiad.

RITA LEISTNER, ARTIST STATEMENT

The Edward Curtis Project began in the summer of 2007. Brenda Leadlay at Presentation House Theatre had asked Métis/Dene playwright Marie Clements to pitch an idea for the 2010 Cultural Olympiad in Vancouver. Marie wanted to write a play about Edward Sheriff Curtis and *The North American Indian* (1900–1930)— his epic and controversial photographic record of America's First Peoples—and she wanted me to undertake a parallel photojournalistic investigation. These photographs are born of a unique collaboration among a playwright, a photojournalist, and many individuals in First Nation communities in Canada and the United States.

It was a commonly held view in Curtis's time that the Aboriginal peoples of North America were a "vanishing race"—and his job was to create a photographic record before it was "too late." But what happens when the "vanishing race" doesn't vanish? What is the impact on a people who are told they are vanishing?

Saying "yes" was the easy part—I was familiar with Clements's powerful, political, and beautiful visual theatre, and I trusted her unreservedly. It was much harder to imagine what kinds of photographs I would make. I had to grapple with the problematic history of representation of First Nation peoples and the havoc Curtis and his colonial contemporaries had wrought. Moreover, in a context where the practice of documentary photography itself was being questioned, I had to craft my reply with the very medium under scrutiny.

Edward Sheriff Curtis was a turn-of-the-century photographer, chronicler, film-maker, anthropologist, and pioneer of the long documentary form in photography who spent thirty years (from 1900 to 1930) working in First Nation communities across North America. His life's work, *The North American Indian*, with its thousands of large-format sepia-toned portraits, as well as interviews and recordings, is both invaluable and problematic to the historical record. As with all art, Curtis's *magnum opus* is also a record of his own subjectivity and the ideas and assumptions of his culture and times. The irony of Curtis's work is that he, his patrons, and those Americans and Europeans who bought his photographs were demonstrating a longing for something they themselves had destroyed. Curtis's complicity with this "imperialist nostalgia," and his lack of interest in social activism is at the heart of the modern controversy over Curtis's work.

And yet Edward Curtis would never have claimed to be anything other than what he was. He was not a photojournalist, and unlike his contemporaries Lewis Hine and Jacob Riis, who pioneered the school of concerned photography, Curtis did not use photography for social reform or to document an accurate and unaltered version of the social injustices he witnessed—such as the growing misery within First Nation communities caused by abusive government policies like the Christian Church-run Residential School system, and the outlawing of regalia and other traditions.

Instead Curtis nostalgically focused on an earlier time, before the white man came to the Americas, when First Nation people still lived among the buffalo. His vision was romantic and pictorial. In order to evoke this idealized past, Curtis borrowed confiscated regalia from museums and government archives, bringing it to remote communities where he and his subjects created elaborately staged tableaus of battles and dances, as well as some of the most powerful and lasting portraits ever made. Curtis was so good at re-enacting the past, he is often erroneously cast as a great nineteenth-century photographer.

As a white photographer photographing First Nation communities, I had something in common with Edward Curtis, yet I was clearly working from a different starting point and within a different tradition than he was. My life's work has been focused on letting my subjects tell the story. Coming from the school of concerned photography, I have always approached my work as a kind of compassionate ethnographer: Not prejudging or having a set plan in place. Each photo, an unknown until it is made, must speak for itself; finally, from a collection of images, a story begins to reveal itself.

In the beginning, Marie and I travelled together to First Nation communities, meeting as many people as we could. With the 2010 Cultural Olympiad deadline looming before us, we had to work quickly. It was exhausting. Two weeks into our fieldwork, needing a break from our search for "the story," we hopped into a pick-up and drove the ice road from Inuvik to Tuktuyuktuk, blasting the Doobie Brothers on the stereo and singing along while Marie's eight-year-old son, Devon, rolled his eyes at us. I took photos of everything—ice, fishing huts, myself, Marie and Devon, a barking sled dog, a boarded-up hotel—not knowing how the story would unfold.

Many months later, when Marie was back home on Galiano Island writing and I was back in the field with my camera, Marie would send me drafts of the play in progress. I thought about the theatricality of Marie's play and how this related to Edward Curtis's elaborate staging. The essential differences are in degrees of control. I can't create characters, I have to go out and meet them. I can't prescribe circumstances and how people think, feel, and act to illustrate a point or opinion. The work is inherently fluid, unpredictable, and ever-changing. Marie's characters were changing and evolving too, and as we all delved deeper into the project, our stories became increasingly intertwined.

Early on I had abandoned the idea of photographing people in regalia à la Edward Curtis. This changed after Marie and I happened upon a theatrical performance in Haida Gwaii, British Columbia. *Sinxii' Gangu* (*Sounding Gambling Sticks*), written by Jaalen and Gwaii Edenshaw, is an original Haida language play featuring local artists who studied the Haida language with elders and language experts. The day after its premiere at Masset High School, enrolment in Haida language classes went way up. "It's made speaking Haida cool again," everyone was saying.

Sinxii' Gangu is an example of the resilience of languages in many First Nation communities and what this generation is doing to recover the heritage that was taken from them. Regalia, and the big comeback its authentic cultural purpose was clearly making in many of the communities we visited, became central to the story of *The Edward Curtis Project.*

The week after I saw *Sinxii' Gangu* (twice), I photographed Jeffrey Williams—who played the lead—in his button blanket and other regalia lent him by his father. I posed Jeff in front of an old truck, wanting to include a symbol of the modern world to distance the work from Curtis, whose portraits intentionally erased any signs of modernity. After the shoot, I drove Jeff home where he quickly changed before going to meet friends in town. A typically fashion-conscious teen, Jeff emerged in rapper-style and I commented on how cool he looked. It was his idea to take a second photograph in his "street clothes costume." That night he posted both images on his Facebook page. And so began the diptych series that became a central motif of *The Edward Curtis Project*—a photographic exploration of past and present, traditional and modern, as presented by the subjects themselves.

Nearly two years after Marie Clements first approached me about *The Edward Curtis Project*, I showed dozens of diptychs, including ones I had just made of Comanche war veterans, to Comanche artist and Methodist lay-minister Timothy Nevaquaya at the Apache, Oklahoma, home of his brother Sonny Nevaquaya, a master flautist. Tim talked to me about the overlap of past and present and how the regalia of today address both. "It's a re-emergence," he said. "When you look at the vests worn by members of the Comanche Indian Veterans Association, it's based on that of the Comanche warriors—the beadwork is a sign of the past, yet it also tells a story of where a person's at in today's world." Comanche war veteran Sergeant Major Lanny Asepermy added: "We don't know exactly what our Comanche warriors wore in the past, and what we do know comes largely from nineteenth-century paintings, and from Edward Curtis's photographs."

As Tim spoke, the haunting sounds of Sonny's flute floated and echoed through the room—the music taught him by his famous father, Doc Tate Nevaquaya, who is widely credited with the renaissance of Native American flute music in the 1970s, after years of its suppression. "This big misunderstanding of our way of life is just like the flute," Tim said. "Had the early settlers understood this marvellous thing they would not have stopped its progression, and there's no telling what could have happened had the flute and its music not become lost. But I think now we're back on the right track."

Gerald McMaster—the celebrated Plains Cree artist and an authority on Edward Curtis—cautioned me early on not to just show the rosy side of life. Dig deep, he'd told me. Tell the truth.

The photographs in this book are mere glimpses into a complex world, yet, like Curtis's Indians, they will move through time and space beyond the moment when they were recorded with a camera. I hope my photographs create a visual dialogue or bridge between past and present, between the legacy of Edward Curtis and the colonial past, and the bright future elucidated by many of the people I met in my travels.

—Rita Leistner

1.
Krista Nicole Hubbard, long-time Comanche Indian Veterans Association (CIVA) Princess. A senior and straight-A student at Eisenhower High School in Lawton, Oklahoma.
Lawton, Oklahoma, USA, November 2009

2.
Petty Officer 1st Class Jimmy Caddo, US Navy (retired), 1952–72, Comanche. Korean and Vietnam Wars. Awarded the Korean War, United Nations, and Vietnam Service Medals, the Vietnam Gallantry Cross, and the Combat Action Ribbon. Apache, Oklahoma, USA, November 2009.

3.
Specialist Eleanor (Atauvich) McDaniel, US Army, 1982–92, Comanche. Member of a five-person weapons/ammo disposal team during Operation Desert Shield and Operation Desert Storm. First Comanche woman to serve in combat and recipient of the Southwest Asia Service Medal with 3 Battle Stars and the Kuwait Liberation Medal.
Cache, Oklahoma, USA, November 2009.

4.
Sergeant Major Lanny Asepermy, US Army (retired), 1966–90, Comanche/Kiowa. Served in Vietnam War, Korean War, and Bosnian conflict. He is the most decorated Comanche Nation veteran, whose fifty awards include the Legion of Merit, Meritorious Service (2), Army Commendation Medals (8), and the Combat Infantryman Badge.
Apache, Oklahoma, USA, November 2009.

5.
Corporal Edmond Mahseet, US Marine Corps, 1964–68, Comanche. Two tours in Vietnam and participated in 26 combat operations—fought and killed the enemy in hand-to-hand combat and was awarded the Combat Action Ribbon (2), the Vietnam Service Medal with 4 Battle Stars, and the Presidential Unit Citation.
Lawton, Oklahoma, USA, November 2009.

6.
Fort Defiance Navajo Veterans Cemetery, where over 600 Navajo veterans are laid to rest, whose military services span from the Indian Wars of the mid-1800s to the Iraq and Afghanistan wars of today. Full to capacity, the cemetery is in urgent need of land and funding for expansion.
Fort Defiance, Navajo Nation, Arizona, USA, July 2008.

7.
Officer Tom Leland of the Navajo Tribal Police, a Vietnam War veteran, comes from a long line of soldiers and motorcycle aficionados.
Rock Springs, Navajo Nation, Arizona, USA, July 2008.

Leland's mother, ninety-nine-year-old Berta Tom, holds an 1899 photograph of her father, Charlie Boyd Watson, who was a survivor of "The Long Walk" (also called "The Trail of Tears"). Thousands of Native Americans died of illness, duress, or starvation as a result of nineteenth-century United States government initiatives to relocate Native Americans, on foot, to Oklahoma. Some, like Tom Leland's grandfather, were able to escape and make the journey back home where they would raise families on the land they hailed from.
Rock Springs, Navajo Nation, Arizona, USA, July 2008.

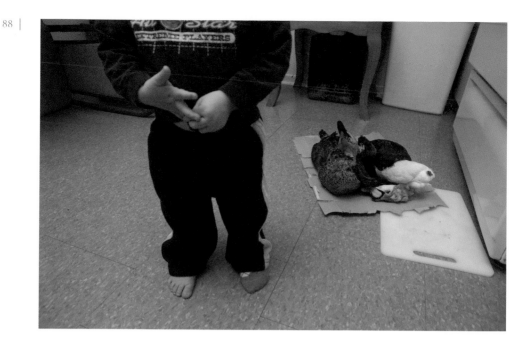

8.
Tobin Klengenberg and King Eider ducks in the kitchen of his parents, Ross and Laverna. The white-headed duck is the male, or "Kingali" in Inuvialuktun. The female is called "Mitac."
Ulukhaktok, Northwest Territories, Canada, September 2009.

A goose in Winnie Akhiatak's kitchen. The hamlet of Ulukhaktok, which means "place where you find ulus"—the sharp slate stones originally used to make the kind of knife on Winnie's knife display—reclaimed its original name in 2006, dropping the European name "Holman."
Ulukhaktok, Northwest Territories, Canada, September 2009.

9.
top: Easter Sunday at the Aklavik Anglican Church.
Aklavik, Northwest Territories, Canada, March 2008.

bottom: Grave markers of repatriated remains of 160 Haida ancestors, mostly children, from the Field Museum in Chicago. Children were stolen from their families and communities as part of the Christian Church-run Indian Residential School system, widely considered a form of cultural genocide.
Old Masset Cemetery, Haida Gwaii, British Columbia, Canada, June 2008.

top: Boarded-up Catholic church.
Ulukhaktok, Northwest Territories, Canada, September 2009.

bottom: Jesuit "igloo" church.
Inuvik, Northwest Territories, Canada, September 2009.

10.
Mary M. Firth's camp in Gwich'in territory.
Eight Mile, Northwest Territories, Canada, September 2009.

Berta Tom's Hogan—a traditional Navajo home with its entrance facing east to welcome the sunrise.
Rock Springs, New Mexico, USA, July 2008.

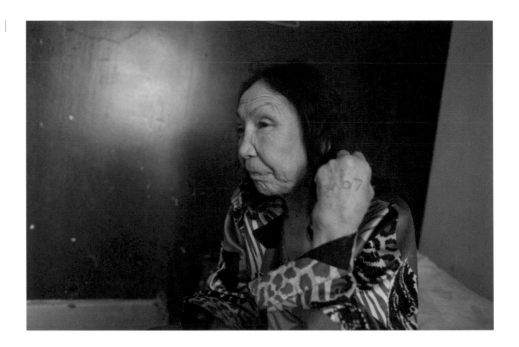

11.

top: Kathy Rattlesnake, longtime resident of Canada's poorest neighbourhood, the Downtown Eastside (DTES) of Vancouver, in her room at the Washington Hotel. Kathy is from the Samson Cree First Nation of Hobbema, Alberta. About one in four residents on the DTES is from a First Nation—nearly eight times the national average.

bottom: The Hotel Empress, one of dozens of single-resident occupancy buildings on the DTES. Shabby single rooms with common bathrooms cost $375.00 per month. Because the money is sent directly from Social Services, there is no motivation to maintain sites. But landlords argue tenants take poor care of the spaces, and they are doing them a favour. Vancouver Downtown Eastside, British Columbia, Canada, March 2009.

top: Deborah Hoyme of Brampton, Ontario, loves Alex Mountain of the Kwaquitl First Nation from Alert Bay, British Columbia. Deborah and Alex grew up on the Downtown Eastside, taking care of parents, friends, and each other.

bottom: Arthur Bear, "Bear" to his friends. A longtime resident of the DTES, Bear, who is Cree, has lived in this 8 x 9 foot room at the Cordova Residence for three years and has a small collection of bears in his tiny but tidy room. Vancouver Downtown Eastside, British Columbia, Canada, March 2009.

12.
top: Navajo sculptor Pete Teller at his home in Rough Rock, surrounded by his work, carved from local stone as well as stone he imports from Italy.
Rough Rock, Navajo Nation, Arizona, USA, July 2008.

bottom: Election signage at a busy highway intersection.
Chinle, Navajo Nation, Arizona, USA, July 2008.

top: Environmentally friendly and energy efficient windmill water pumps are a common feature of the landscape in the Navajo Nation, and are overseen by the Navajo Nation Tribal Utility Authority.

bottom: Pete Teller (left) and Navajo painter Joe Vincent Shirley cool off in the forty-degree summer heat. Navajo Nation, Arizona, USA, July 2008.

13.
top: "Zoo York."
Aklavik, Northwest Territories, Canada, March 2008.

bottom: Warming tent at the Mad Trapper Winter Carnival.
Aklavik, Northwest Territories, Canada, March 2008.

top: "West Side."
Ulukhaktok, Northwest Territories, Canada, September 2009.

bottom: Siren tower.
Chinle, Navajo Nation, Arizona, USA, July 2008.

14.

top: Moose antlers, Inuvialuit elder Olive Itis's house.
Fort McPherson, Northwest Territories, Canada, September 2009.

bottom: Moose antlers, Gwich'in elder Ruth Furlong's house.
Aklavik, Northwest Territories, Canada, March 2008.

top: Moose antlers, Gwich'in elder Bernice Francis's house.
Fort McPherson, Northwest Territories, Canada, September 2009.

bottom: Muskox horns, Winnie Akhiatak's shed.
Ulukhaktok, Northwest Territories, Canada, September 2009.

15.
Photographs of Buffalo Bill Cody and Sitting Bull at the Buffalo Bill Museum.
Le Claire, Iowa, USA, July 2008.

Filmmaker Jadal Q'egenga Andersen in her prom dress on Cemetery Beach the day after her graduation from Masset High School, where she was the top recipient of awards for academic achievement.
Masset, Haida Gwaii, British Columbia, Canada, June 2008.

16.

top: Caroline Kay (left) and her younger sister Alice Blake visit youngest sister Mary M. Firth at her camp at Eight Mile (eight miles from Fort McPherson—"Tetlit Zheh" or "The Headwaters" in Gwich'in). Mary has a house in town, but like most Gwich'in elders, she much prefers spending time at her camp and closer to the land.

bottom: Mary M. Firth looks at a book of photographs made by Rita Leistner of clam-diggers in Haida Gwaii as part of *The Edward Curtis Project*.

Eight Mile, Northwest Territories, Canada, September 2009.

top: A rare and happy opportunity for all three sisters to be together.

bottom: After we leave, Mary takes a rest before embarking on the job of butchering fresh moose brought by her son, who visits every day.

17.
Annual February 14th Women's Memorial March to honour over eighty, mostly First Nation, women murdered or missing from the Downtown Eastside.
Vancouver Downtown Eastside, British Columbia, Canada, February 2009.

18.
"My Space" neighbourhood exhibition at W2. Marvin Dennis (left) of the Small Frog First Nation, and Gary Donaldson
of the Tsimshian First Nation, both residents of the Downtown Eastside of Vancouver, look at photographs of themselves

and their friends, in an exhibition on the DTES of photographs (and gifts) made by Rita Leistner as part of *The Edward Curtis Project*, with help from the Vancouver Area Network of Drug Users, Julia Wilson, and Paul Campbell. Vancouver Downtown Eastside, British Columbia, Canada, July 2009.

19.
Jeffrey Williams, lead actor in the Haida language play *Sinxii' Gangu* (*Sounding Gambling Sticks*), which was written by Jaalen and Gwaii Edenshaw with the guidance of Masset Haida language speakers, and produced by Jenny Nelson. Old Masset, Haida Gwaii, British Columbia, Canada, June 2008.

20.
Margaret Egutak, who is skilled at needlework and sewing with furs and cloth, and who made the parka and moccasins she is wearing, was born on the land in an igloo, on the east side of Banks Island near Sachs Harbour in 1917. Ulukhaktok, Northwest Territories, Canada, September 2009.

21.
Gwaii Edenshaw, whose Haida name is Hluugiilgaa is a sculptor and playwright who co-wrote, with his brother Jaalen, the Haida language play *Sinxii' Gangu* (*Sounding Gambling Sticks*), with help from Masset Haida language speakers. His mother, Jenny Nelson, produced the play.
Tow Hill, Haida Gwaii, British Columbia, Canada, June 2008.

22.
Erika Stocker wearing her favourite rain boots and her Haida blanket, which she received in the traditional way, as a rite of passage on the eve of her graduation from Masset High School a few days before these photos were taken. Erika received a 2008 YVR (Vancouver Airport) Art Foundation Scholarship.
Tow Hill, Haida Gwaii, British Columbia, Canada, June 2008.

23.
Ida Kuneyuna, who is skilled at needlework and sewing with furs and cloth, and who made the parkas and moccasins she is wearing, was born in an igloo, near Reed Island on the far side of Albert Sound in 1937.
Ulukhaktok, Northwest Territories, Canada, September 2009.

24.
Tiffany Vanderhoop, Haida textile artist, of Masset, British Columbia, and Aquinnah, Massachusetts. Tiffany's great-great-grandfather was photographed by Edward Curtis.
Tow Hill, Haida Gwaii, British Columbia, Canada, June 2008.

25.
Sean Brennan, Haida carver, atop logs he is carving to build a longhouse with his father-in-law, master Haida carver Cooper Wilson.
Old Masset, Haida Gwaii, British Columbia, Canada, June 2008.

26.
Ross Klengenberg, Inuvialuit sculptor, hunter, and trapper with his new Ski-Doo and wearing a parka that his mother made and that had been worn by his father before him.
Ulukhaktok, Northwest Territories, Canada, September 2009.

27.
Raven Ann Potschka, Haida artist, activist, and actor.
Masset, Haida Gwaii, British Columbia, Canada, June 2008.

28.
Jack Nokalak Akhiatak, Inuvialuit hunter and trapper.
Ulukhaktok, Northwest Territories, Canada, September 2009.

29.
Sergeant Dominic G. Lafontaine, US Army, 1988–present, Navajo. Iraq War (2005, 2007, 2008). When on leave from the military, Court Bailiff Lafontaine serves with the Navajo Tribal Police. Photographed in front of the Navajo Nation Veterans Memorial.
Window Rock, Navajo Nation, Arizona, USA, July 2008.

30.
Adam Kudlak, volunteer firefighter and traditional Inuvialuit ulu knife-maker.
Ulukhaktok, Northwest Territories, Canada, September 2009.

Fred Akoaksion, volunteer firefighter and traditional Inuvialuit drum-dancer.
Ulukhaktok, Northwest Territories, Canada, September 2009.

31.
Joseph Drager of the Haida First Nation digs for clams on the Pacific Coast. Clam-digging, an ancient food harvesting practice among the Haida, has been stymied by Fisheries and Oceans Canada quotas and declining prices. Drager has several other jobs, including one collecting remaindered wood (such as rejects from logging companies) from the coastal rainforest.
Tow Hill Beach, Haida Gwaii, British Columbia, Canada, June 2008.

Haida entrepreneur Joey Parnell runs several businesses, including a clam-digging crew and a wood reclamation outfit, employing many young men in the community, including Joseph Drager (left).
Tow Hill Beach, Haida Gwaii, British Columbia, Canada, June 2008.

32.
Caroline Kay, walking along the shore of the Peel River, enjoys taking in the scenery and sharing memories of a life on the land. Caroline was born on New Year's Eve, 1914, out on the land in the Yukon. Her parents and thirteen brothers and sisters used to make the sometimes weeks-long trip by canoe up the river to Fort McPherson.
Peel River, Fort McPherson, Northwest Territories, Canada, September 2009.

Edward Curtis Project playwright Marie Clements's aunt, Ruth Furlong, at her home in Aklavik. The cold of winter is a particularly difficult time for elders who find few opportunities to get out of the house. The joy of our visit also brought on the melancholy of our departure.
Aklavik, Northwest Territories, Canada, March 2008.

Aunt Ruth passed away in April 2009 surrounded by her family. This exhibition is in part dedicated to her memory.

33.
Cooper Wilson in his atelier/trailer where the master Haida carver has apprenticed many carvers in the community who have gone on to become established artists.

Deer hanging in front of Haida artist Chris White's longhouse, a hub of artistic, cultural, and traditional activities in the community.
Old Masset, Haida Gwaii, British Columbia, Canada, June 2008.

34.
"Baby Cakes," a victim of domestic violence, finds comfort and safety at the home of surrogate parents Dorrinda Disney
and Nick Brown.
Old Masset, Haida Gwaii, British Columbia, Canada, June 2008.

35.
Muskox hunting with brothers Earl and Jack Akhiatak and Jack's wife, Irene. That day it took a while to find a small enough muskox. The big ones are tough to eat, and only interesting to trophy hunters from the south. The Inuvialuit use every part of the muskox for food and clothing and share generously with the whole community.
Anyyaluk, Northwest Territories, Canada, September 2009.

All the cleaning and primary butchering is done in the field, masterfully, by Earl, Jack, and Irene. Everything is tied into the skin in a big bundle and towed to the edge of the Beaufort Sea for its five-hour boat trip home to Ulukhaktok.

36.
Agnes Kuptana and her husband Robert are renowned Inuvialuit translators and interpreters of the Inuvialuktun and English languages.
Ulukhaktok, Northwest Territories, Canada, September 2009.

37.
Leo Gagnon, master Haida carver and mentor to many community youth, in front of his house, with stripped cedar bark used for weaving.
Old Masset, Haida Gwaii, British Columbia, Canada, June 2008.

38. Crew Shot 1.

top: *Edward Curtis Project* photographer Rita Leistner in her room at the Lotus Hotel on Vancouver's Downtown Eastside. Special thanks to Mark James, who owns the Lotus Hotel and offered her the room for a month, in exchange for photography, so she would have an opportunity to live close to the people she was photographing.
Vancouver Downtown Eastside, British Columbia, Canada, March 2009.

bottom: *Edward Curtis Project* playwright Marie Clements and her video camera at an old abandoned gas station where we stopped to stretch our legs after a long drive.
Fort Garland, New Mexico, USA, July 2008.

top: Marie Clements and her nephew Arthur Georgeson enjoy the invigorating climate (minus forty degrees) at the Mad Trapper Winter Carnival.
Aklavik, Northwest Territories, Canada, March 2008.

bottom: Lena Nigiyok and Brittany Akoaksion showed me how to golf on the tundra (I am really bad at golf), while I showed them how to use my Canon Mark II digital SLR (and actually their photos were pretty good!)
Ulukhaktok, Northwest Territories, Canada, September 2009.

39. Crew Shot 2

top: Marie Clements, her son Devon, and her nephew Arthur board the plane to Inuvik after a stop-over in Norman Wells on the way from Yellowknife, on the way from Edmonton, on the way from Vancouver.
Norman Wells Airport (YVQ), Northwest Territories, Canada, March 2008.

bottom: Devon and Arthur, who are angelic, make snow angels on the Mackenzie River ice road.
Near Aklavik, Northwest Territories, Canada, March 2008.

top: (left to right) Arthur Georgeson, Marie Clements, and Devon Zobatar. The fabulous Rosemarie Georgeson, our field producer in the Arctic and in Vancouver, who is also Marie's cousin, and the Aboriginal community director of urban ink productions. Cousins Archie and Rita Arey, who live in Aklavik, and their grandson Connor. Filmmaker and the coolest member of our crew, Richard Wilson, who is also Marie and Rose's cousin.

bottom: Marie and Richard making themselves at home at a trapper's camp on the Mackenzie River. Near Aklavik, Northwest Territories, Canada, March 2008.

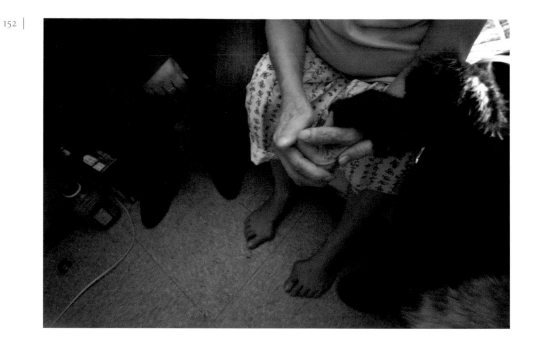

40. Crew Shot 3: Saying good-bye to family and friends in Aklavik, Northwest Territories.
top: Ruth Furlong.

bottom: Our crew with Florence Furlong and Charlie Furlong, then president of the Gwich'in Tribal Council.

top: Rancher and raconteur R.V. Robertson entertains Marie, Rita, and Rhiana Yazzie, upcoming Navajo playwright who joined us in the Southern Plains.
White Mountain Trading Post, Fort Garland, New Mexico, USA, July 2008.

bottom: Marie and Rhiana at Indian City Campground, Oklahoma, USA, 2008.

41. Crew Shot 4
Rita Leistner and Scott Chisel Stephens at the Southern Plains Museum in Anadarko, Oklahoma. Scott, an outstanding, talented, upcoming Anishnabe photographer based in Winnipeg, hopes to embed with Canadian troops in Afghanistan. When Scott asked me if he could do a mentorship with me, I suggested he join me in Oklahoma where I'd be spending time with Comanche war veterans as part of *The Edward Curtis Project*.

top: Scott is in conversation with Comanche war veteran Edmond Mahseet.

bottom: Comanche war veteran Lanny Asepermy has done more than any individual, through film, museums, and memorials, to keep alive the memory of Comanche war veterans. He and his wife Shelley welcomed us like family. My photos of Comanche war vets could not have been made without their unwavering support of my work in *The Edward Curtis Project Exhibition*.
Anadarko and Apache, Oklahoma, USA, November 2009.

42. Crew Shot 5

top: Invaluable contributions to *The Edward Curtis Project Exhibition* were made on the Downtown Eastside by Paul Campbell (left), SFU scholar Julia Wilson (on floor); Marvin Dennis, Clyde, and Rick (and many others!), videographer Andrew Lavigne. W2 Gallery courtesy of Irwin Oostinde. Prints at W2 courtesy of PacBlue. DTES Vancouver, British Columbia, Canada, July 2009.

bottom: The send-off brunch: Brenda Leadlay, Presentation House Theatre artistic director and the producer behind *The Edward Curtis Project* (standing). Joining Brenda, Marie, and Rita for brunch is Gerald McMaster, acclaimed Cree artist, member of the Order of Canada, and director of Canadian exhibitions at the Art Gallery of Ontario, who was in Vancouver giving a presentation on Edward Curtis.

Vancouver, British Columbia, Canada, March 2008.

THANKS

The Edward Curtis Project would have been impossible without the kindness and generosity of many people—friends, family, and colleagues from home as well as new friends we met along the way. We are grateful to you all.

Kevin and Vicki Williams and Christy and Karl Siegler at Talonbooks had the vision to keep *The Edward Curtis Project* play and exhibition together in a published book. The team at Talonbooks, including Garry Thomas Morse and Gregory Gibson, have been wonderful. Thank you for this book!

Thanks to our producer, Brenda Leadlay, at Presentation House Theatre, dramaturge Paula Danckert, Nancy Kirkpatrick of the North Vancouver Museum, who mounted the exhibition; *The Edward Curtis Project* core production and field crew, including Rosemary Georgeson, Rhiana Yazzie, Richard Wilson, Arthur Georgeson, Devon Zobatar, Jackie Gow, Susan Roy, Barbara Clayden; our incredible cast and design team including Kathleen Duboig, Stephen E. Miller, Kevin Loring, Tamara Podemski, Bruce Ruddell, Leela Gilday, John Webber, Tim Matheson, and Andreas Kahre; as well as our production and stage management team including Jan Hodgson, Karen Griffin, Gia Nahmens, Liam Kupser, Katarzyna Marzencka, Jack Hendry, translator Zalmai Zahir, Presentation House Theatre general manager Neil Scott, and PHT's Alise Bennner and Graham Howard.

Special thanks to Henry and Joan Leistner and Donna Leistner, Saify Khan, Rob Zobatar, Aaron Glass, the Akhiatak family, Alison Nordstrom and the George Eastman House, Brenda Hanson and Family, Bill Macdonald, Bonnie MacGillivary, Brian Green, Cecil Halsey, Christopher and Lara Morris, Char Tullie, Dan Savard, Debra Prince, Don Bourdon, Emma Tibaldo, Evelyn Zobatar, Femke Van Delft, Florence Furlong, Gerald McMaster, Gina Wilson, Glen Morrow, Lucien Durey, Irwin Oostindie, Jadai q'ĝongó Andersen, Jenny Amour, Mari Chijiiwa, Julia Wilson, Ken Cameron, Lanny and Shelley Asepermy, Mugu lla North Festival, Mark James, Martha Black, Nial McNeil, Michelle St. John, Naomi Campbell, Nick Westover, Norman Armour, Pac Blue Printing in Vancouver, Patricia Matson, Paul Campbell, Paul Grech, Pete Teller, PUSH Festival, Redux Pictures, R.V. and Melana Robertson, and Scott "Chisel" Stephens, Sherrie Johnson, Taddoussac Playwright's Residence, Terry Lynn Williams-Davidson, Thomas Kellog, and Zalmai Zabir.

For friendship, invaluable support, emergency phone calls, and help editing thousands of photographs, thanks to Steve Simon, Alan Chin, Arthur Gottschalk, Bonnie and Fred Warrilow, Bree Seeley, Chris Decherd, Corinne Seiler, Dale

McMurchy, Daniel MacIvor, Dolores Gubasta, Doug Nicholson, Guntar Kravis, Diana Kuprel, Henry Knight, Iris Turcott, Jamie Wellford, John Trotter, Kate Anthony and Pam Walker, Katja Heinemann, Kay Koppedrayer, Kendall Messick, Kisha Ferguson, Lesley Robertson, Lesley Sparks, Lin Stranberg, Lawrence Cook, Lianne Scott and Patrick Sipos, Louie Palu, Lesley Sparks, Linda, Daniel, Stefan and Melanie Leistner, Martin and Raja Leistner, Paul and Pam Warrilow, Melissa Williams, Natalie Matutschovsky, Phillip S. Block and The International Centre for Photography, Peter Gyles, Robert Blake, Robert Palmer, Teru Kuwayama, Tina Baylis and family, Tobi Asmoucha and William Marsden.

Bob Carnie and Kevin Viner at ELEVATOR Digital in Toronto did an amazing job printing and framing the exhibition.

In the course of our travels to communities in Haida Gwaii, the Western Canadian Arctic, Vancouver's Downtown Eastside, Arizona, New Mexico, and Oklahoma, USA, we met hundreds of people and made thousands of photographs. We are touched and honoured by the kindness and trust shown us by so many:

Ulukhaktok, Northwest Territories: Albert and Shirley Elias, Andy and Mary, Annie Oloakyok, Danny Taptuna, David and Bella Kuptana, Denise Okheena, Donna Akhiatak, Earl Akhiatak, Emily Kudlak, Fred and Trudy-Anne Akoaksion, Ida Kuneyuna, Irene Akhiatak, Isaac Kataoyak, Jack Kataoyak, Joane Ogina, Laverna, Ross, Carmell, and Tobin Klengenberg, Margaret Egotak, Mary Akoaksion, Melanie Kudlak, Noah Akhiatiac, Robert and Agnes Kuptana, Winnie Akhiatak.

Aklavik, Northwest Territories: The Furlong family, Archie Arey and Rita Arey, Charlie Furlong, Dane Gibson, Dean McLeod, Dorothy Erigatoak, Ruth Furlong, Mary Kendi, Principal Velma Illisiak and the students and teachers of the Moose Kerr School.

Inuvik, Northwest Territories: Angela Young, Eugene Reese, John Holman, Lee Mason, Martin Landry, Paul Grech, Topsy Cockney, Victor Stewart, the Ten A.M. Coffee Club at the Gallery Café, the students and teachers of Samuel Hearne Secondary School.

Fort McPherson, Northwest Territories: Alice Blake, Caroline Kay, David Cook, Mary F. Firth.

Yellowknife, Northwest Territories: George Tuccaro, James Jenka, John Rombough, William S. Greenland.

Haida Gwaii, British Columbia: Aggie, Sam and Helen Davis at Nonnie's B&B, Adina Young, Angela Long, Archie and Liz Stocker, Archie and Mandy Andersen, Candace Weir-White and Christian White, Cherie Wilson, Cooper Wilson, Cynthia Davidson, Daniel Bell, Dempsey Bell, Dorrinda Disney, Eddie Williams, Elizabeth Moore, Erika Raelene (Stocker), Frazer, Gerry Johnson, Grand Chief Guujaaw Edenshaw, Gwaii Edenshaw, Jack Litrell, Jaalen Edenshaw, Jaret Parnell, Jason Major, Jeffrey Williams, Jenny Nelson, Jin Chong, Jody Russ, Joey Parnell, John Parnell, Joseph Drager, Ken Rea, Leo Gagnon, Lucy Bell, Meredith Adams and family, Marlene Little, Maxine Edgars, Meredith Adams and family, Nathalie Macfarlane at the Haida Heritage Centre, Norman, Randy Martin, Randy Russ, Raven Ann Potschka, Raymond Jones, Roy Collison, Robert Watts, Sean Brennan, Sheri Burton, Swarn

Hollington, Tiffany Lavoie, Tiffany Vanderhoop, Tony Brown, Trevor Russ, Verne Brown, Warren MacIntyre, Wilfred Bell, everyone at The Copper Beach House and the Moon Over Nikoon.

Arizona and New Mexico: Berta Tom, Pastor Bob, Carol Palmer, Char Tullie and Robert Johnson at the Navajo Nation Museum, Sgt. Daren Simeone, Daryl Shack, David Jordan, Deenise Becenti, Earl Millfort, Frances Yazzie, George Hardeen, Jamie Billie, Marilyn Dempsey, Elizabeth Dempsey, Officer Nick Lafontaine, Peter Teller, Roberta Roberts, Ronald P. Maldonado, Capt. Ronny Wanika, RV and Melana Robertson and family, Samantha Yazzie, Capt. Steve Nelson, Steven Begay, Officer Tom Leland, Vincent Joe Shirley

Vancouver, British Columbia: Adella Zeller, Alex Mountain, Alwin Benson, Andrew Lavigne, April Smith, Arthur Bear, Brian Frasier, Bud Osborne, Carol Martin, Cecily Nicholson, Christine Germano, Clyde Wright, Cody Georgeson, Curtis and Floyd, Dale Dingman, Dan and Deb, Dan Cottie, Dave Wilson, Deborah Hoyme, Derek Dean, Femke van Delft, Fern Charlie, Gary Donaldson, Harold Alashan, Hector Ritch, Hendrik Beune, Holly Boyd, Jacky, Johnny Roy "Bingo" Dawson, Juanita, Kathy Rattlesnake, Kevin Annet, Larry Bull, Lucie Landry, Lyle Thompson, Marvin Dennis, Mike Desjarlais, Molly Fanny, Nancy Bleck, Nick Collins, Nicole Lytham, the Out to Lunch Bunch, Paul Campbell, Paul Ryan, Penny Wells, Peter Thompson, Priscilla Tait and the DTES Women Writers Group, Reta Blind and the Sweetgrass Place, Rick Alexander, Rick C., Rose Humphrey, Stan Paul, Steve and friends at The Carnegie, Steven Tong, Susie Gray and Mylo Ryley, Thea Walters and Mora at LINES, Tim Bonham.

Ladner, British Columbia: Ken Turpin, Mike Crocker, Chief Rocky Wilson, and Rosalie Wilson.

Apache, Oklahoma: The Comanche Indian Veterans Association (CIVA) and members Edmund and Elizabeth Maliscet, Eleanor McDaniel, George Red Elk, Jimmy and Beverly Caddo, Krista Nicole Hubbard and Susie and her parents Frank Hubbard, Lanny and Shelley Asepermy, Sunny Nevaquaya and Timothy Nevaquaya; Venessa Paukeigope Jenning, and Phyllis Wahahrockah-Tasi at the Comanche National Museum.

Our sincere apologies to anyone we have forgotten.

—in spirit, Marie Clements and Rita Leistner